Merry Christmas!

MERRY CHRISTMAS!

A History of the Holiday

By PATRICIA BUNNING STEVENS

MACMILLAN PUBLISHING CO., INC.
New York

COLLIER MACMILLAN PUBLISHERS
London

Grateful acknowledgement is made to the following for permission to quote material: The translation of "Hymn to the Sun" on page 23 is reprinted by permission of the translator, Florence Marie Gerdes, C.S.J.; the translation of "O Tannenbaum" on page 91 is reprinted by permission of Prentice-Hall, Inc. Englewood Cliffs, New Jersey, from *The International Book of Christmas Carols* (pages 138-139) by Walter Ehret and George K. Evans, © 1963; the broadcast description of the Christmas truce in France, 1914, on page 132 is reprinted by permission of The British Broadcasting Corporation from *The Twelve Days of Christmas* by Miles and John Hadfield (Little, Brown and Company, Boston), Copyright © 1961 by Miles and John Hadfield; the excerpt from *The Death of Christmas: Interviews With Forty-Three Survivors* (Follett Publishing Company, Chicago, 1971) on page 134 is reprinted by permission of Cook County's Neediest Families Christmas Fund, sponsored by the Illinois Department of Public Aid, The First National Bank and Cook County, Illinois.

Macmillan Publishing Co., Inc.
866 Third Avenue, New York, N.Y. 10022
Collier Macmillan Canada, Ltd.

Printed in the United States of America

10 9 8 7 6 5 4 3 2 1

LIBRARY OF CONGRESS CATALOGING IN PUBLICATION DATA

Stevens, Patricia Bunning.
Merry Christmas! : A history of the holiday.
Bibliography: p.
Includes index.
SUMMARY: Traces the history and development of the Christmas holiday from ancient pagan festivals to contemporary American celebrations.
1. Christmas–History–Juvenile literature. 2. Christmas–United States–History–Juvenile literature. [1. Christmas–History] I. Title.
GT4985.S76 394.2'68282'09 79-13762
ISBN 0-02-788210-1

In memory of my father,
John William Bunning,
and to my mother,
Mayme Spencer Bunning

My sincerest thanks to all who helped me in my quest for information, including Cecilia Crowley of the La Grange Public Library, Katherine Kennicott Davis, Paul Ecke, Sr. Florence Marie Gerdes, C.S.J., and Linton Pitluga.

I am especially grateful for the courtesy shown me by Robert May, who was most gracious and helpful though he was ill and home-bound. Mr. May died on August 11, 1976. I believe I was the last person to interview him about his beloved Rudolph.

My thanks, too, to my ever patient editor, Phyllis Larkin.

PATRICIA BUNNING STEVENS

Contents

Merry Christmas!

Introduction

CHRISTMAS. The very word evokes a dozen images, stirs up a hundred memories. What is Christmas?

It is a stable, and a child, and a message of joy and hope that has gone ringing down through two thousand years. It can be no less, yet it is also more.

It is gaiety, gifts and greetings, a winter holiday with roots that stretch far back in human history. It is the Old World of long, long ago, for Egypt, Mesopotamia, Greece, Rome and the fierce barbarian tribes of northern Europe all helped to shape the day. It is Saturn and Daghda, Berchta and Frey, for much of the homage once paid the old pagan gods and goddesses has come to center on the little Christian Prince of Peace. It is the wreath on the door, the tree in the window, the mistletoe hanging from the ceiling. It is song, it is love, it is laughter, all that is good in life itself.

Where can such a story begin? Surely it must begin with the birth of a child in Bethlehem.

O LITTLE TOWN OF BETHLEHEM

O little town of Bethlehem,
How still we see thee lie;
Above thy deep and dreamless sleep
The silent stars go by.
Yet in thy dark streets shineth
The everlasting Light;
The hopes and fears of all the years
Are met in thee tonight.

For Christ is born of Mary;
And gathered all above,
While mortals sleep, the angels keep
Their watch of wondering love.
O morning stars, together
Proclaim the holy birth;
And praises sing to God the King,
And peace to men on earth!

How silently, how silently
The wondrous gift is given!
So God imparts to human hearts
The blessings of His heaven.

No ear may hear His coming,
  But in this world of sin,
Where meek souls will receive Him, still
  The dear Christ enters in.

PHILLIPS BROOKS, 1868

A Child Is Born

LUKE 2:1–20

In those days a decree went out from Caesar Augustus that all the world should be enrolled. This was the first enrollment, when Quirinius was governor of Syria. And all went to be enrolled, each to his own city. And Joseph also went up from Galilee, from the city of Nazareth, to Judea, to the city of David, which is called Bethlehem, because he was of the house and lineage of David, to be enrolled with Mary, his betrothed, who was with child. And while they were there, the time came for her to be delivered. And she gave birth to her first-born son and wrapped him in swaddling cloths, and laid him in a manger, because there was no place for them in the inn.

And in that region there were shepherds out in the field, keeping watch over their flocks by night. And an angel of the Lord appeared to them, and the glory of the Lord shone around them, and they were filled with fear. And the angel said to them, "Be not afraid, for behold, I bring you good news of a great joy which will come to all the people; for to you is born this day in the city of David a Savior, who is Christ the Lord. And this will be a sign for you: you will find a babe wrapped in swaddling cloths and lying in a manger." And suddenly there was with the angel a multitude of the heavenly host praising God, and saying,

> "Glory to God in the highest, and on earth peace
> among men with whom he is pleased."*

When the angels went away from them into heaven, the shepherds said to one another, "Let us go over to Bethlehem and see this thing that has happened which the Lord has made known to us." And they went with haste, and found Mary and Joseph, and the babe lying in a manger. And when they saw it they made known the saying which had been told them concerning this child, and all who heard it wondered at what the shepherds told them. But Mary kept all these things, pondering them in her heart. And the shepherds returned, glorifying and praising God for all they had heard and seen, as it had been told them.

Matthew 2:1–12

Now when Jesus was born in Bethlehem of Judea in the days of Herod the king, behold, wise men from the East came to Jerusalem, saying, "Where is he who has been born king of the Jews? For we have seen his star in the East, and have come to worship him." When Herod the king heard this, he was troubled, and all Jerusalem with him; and assembling all the chief priests and scribes of the people, he inquired of them where the Christ was to be born. They told him, "In Bethlehem of Judea; for so it is written by the prophet:

> 'And you, O Bethlehem, in the land of Judah,
> are by no means least among the rulers of Judah;
> for from you shall come a ruler
> who will govern my people Israel.' "

Then Herod summoned the wise men secretly and ascertained from them what time the star appeared; and he sent

* Other ancient authorities read "peace, goodwill among men."

them to Bethlehem saying, "Go and search diligently for the child, and when you have found him bring me word, that I too may come and worship him." When they had heard the king they went their way; and lo, the star which they had seen in the East went before them till it came to rest over the place where the child was. When they saw the star, they rejoiced exceedingly with great joy; and going into the house they saw the child with Mary his mother, and they fell down and worshiped him. Then, opening their treasures, they offered him gifts, gold and frankincense and myrrh. And being warned in a dream not to return to Herod, they departed to their own country by another way.

Almost all that is known about the birth of Jesus Christ is told in these brief passages from the gospels. Without them, there would be no Christmas. There might be a great midwinter feast. Indeed, there undoubtedly would be a great midwinter feast; but without at least some knowledge of the birth of Christ, it could not be Christmas.

Of the four men who wrote the gospels—Matthew, Mark, Luke and John—only two tell us anything about the Nativity. To the first Christians the important part of the gospel, the "good news," was Christ's teachings and resurrection. Perhaps with so much to tell, Mark and John simply did not think Christ's birth was important enough to write about.

It is Luke who tells us the most about the birth. He must have gotten his information from someone who was there, someone who could remember the tiny details like the swaddling cloths and the manger. The fact that his narrative includes phrases like "Mary kept all these things, pondering them in her heart" has led some scholars to believe that Mary herself may have been his source, or that the story was passed on to Luke by someone who had been very close to her.

It is Matthew alone who records the visit of the wise men, the Magi. He may have wanted to stress right at the start of his gospel that this was a very special child, one whom important people from other countries honored and a king feared.

Where was Christ born? Though Luke and Matthew chose to include two entirely different sets of details in their gospel narratives, both emphasize that Jesus was born in Bethlehem, a tiny village in Judea. Judea was the southernmost part of a larger area known as Palestine, which for centuries had been the homeland of the Jews—the "chosen people" of the Old Testament, the descendants of Jacob, the people of Israel.

By the time of Christ's birth, the Jews had lost all of their political power. Rome, now a great empire ruled by Caesar Augustus, dominated the ancient world. Palestine was governed for Rome by a puppet king, Herod, who was an Idumean by birth. He had little real loyalty to either the Romans or the Jews, but he was determined to keep his throne.

The Jews, unhappy with this foreign domination, turned to the writings of the early prophets. A Messiah had been foretold, who would redeem the people. Now the Jews hoped that this promised savior would be a military leader who would drive out the Roman conquerors and restore the Kingdom of Israel to its ancient glory.

When was Christ born? The question is simple, yet the answer is surprisingly complex. Neither Luke nor Matthew answer it directly. In the first centuries after Christ, when the exact date would have been relatively easy to figure out, no one bothered. The earliest Christians believed that the end of the world was coming soon, perhaps even in their own lifetimes. To them the question would have seemed unimportant, even trivial. And for the followers of Christ the next several hundred years were filled with persecutions, and then with attempts to control differing, quarreling groups that sprang up within the newly established church.

It was not until the sixth century that a monk named Dionysius Exiguus (Dennis the Little, in English) made the calculation that became the basis for our calendar. Before that the years had been counted from the founding of Rome.

Modern chronology begins with 1 A.D., the year in which Dennis believed that Christ was born. A.D. stands for *anno Domini*, the Latin words which mean "the year of the Lord." The years "before Christ" (B.C.) are counted backward, 1 B.C. being the year before Christ's birth, 2 B.C. being two years before, and so on. Unfortunately, Dennis miscalculated. Christ probably was born several years earlier than he believed. By the time this was realized, Dennis's new Christian calendar had been accepted in the western world, and it was too difficult to change it again.

How do we know that Dennis miscalculated? Turning back to the gospels, Matthew tells us that Jesus was born "in the days of Herod the king." Herod died in the spring of 4 B.C., so Christ must have been born before that date. The problem is, how much earlier? Matthew says that Herod, hoping to destroy the infant king before he could become a threat to his own throne, had "killed all the male children in Bethlehem and in all that region who were two years old or under, according to the time which he had ascertained from the wise men." No doubt Herod allowed a generous margin for error in the ages of the children covered by his murderous order. On the other hand, the visit of the wise men and the subsequent slaughter in Bethlehem must have taken place several months before Herod's death. Herod died in Jericho after an illness of some duration, but he apparently was well and certainly was still living in Jerusalem when the wise men came. On the basis of Matthew's information, then, Christ must have been born approximately two years before Herod died, probably in 6 B.C.

Luke's clues are more difficult to trace, but they lead to substantially the same conclusion. The reference to Quirinius is of little help, as we do not know exactly when he first went to Syria. We do know that a census (more properly a registration to make sure that everyone paid taxes) was ordered by the imperial government in Rome in 8 B.C. It was not the first in the empire, but it may well have been the first "enrollment" in an out-of-the-way province like Palestine. The Romans could be ruthlessly efficient, but their bureaucracy, lacking modern communication, moved slowly. Two years would be about the right amount of time for an imperial order to reach a distant province and be put into effect. Luke's information, like Matthew's, points to 6 B.C. as the probable date.

Was Jesus born on December 25? There is no reason to think so. The gospels give no hint at all as to the time of the year; and the day, as we shall see, was chosen at a much later date for reasons that had nothing to do with the actual events in Bethlehem.

Perhaps the month and the day do not really matter. What is important is that two people had left their home in Nazareth and were journeying to Bethlehem in obedience to the law. It is doubtful that travelers meeting them on the road would have noticed anything unusual about them.

Mary, soon to become a mother, was quite young—most likely about sixteen. Jewish girls at that time usually married in their early teens, and sixteen was the most common age for marriage. She may have been even younger.

Joseph was older, but probably not the aged, graying man so often portrayed by medieval artists. Matthew, in a later chapter, speaks of him as a carpenter. The word at the time could mean one who works with stone as well as with wood.

Much has been made of the poverty of the Holy Family, but to the people of their own time they would not have seemed particularly poor. Joseph, as a craftsman, could command far better wages than an unskilled peasant. Furthermore, vast building schemes instituted by Herod had created a demand for skilled workers. Joseph would have been able to find work wherever he went.

No contemporary portraits of the Holy Family exist, nor is it at all likely that any ever were drawn, but the clothing often shown in later paintings probably is accurate. At that time both men and women wore long, seamless tunics, belted or sashed at the waist. In cool weather, a cloak was worn over the tunic. Sandals were customary, and women kept their hair covered in public with some sort of veil or shawl.

Traditionally, Mary is shown riding a donkey with Joseph walking beside her. The portrayal probably is correct. Joseph could have afforded a single beast of burden of some sort, and would have found one useful in his work. If there was only one animal, Mary would have ridden while Joseph walked. Such was the custom of the Jews. In most pagan lands the roles would have been reversed.

The distance from Nazareth to Bethlehem was ninety miles —a long, hard, four-day journey for those who traveled on foot. Yet it is possible that this particular young couple welcomed the trip. Both Mary and Joseph believed that the expected child was destined to be the longed-for Messiah. Very likely they both remembered the words of the prophet Micah which foretold that the future ruler of Israel would come from Bethlehem. Now, thanks to the Roman edict for enrollment, the child would be born in that tiny village.

They apparently arrived late at night. Luke says there was "no room for them in the inn." Tradition has made much of the innkeeper's cruelty and hardness of heart, but Luke's blunt statement of fact does not justify this. The inn would have been crowded with travelers coming to Bethlehem for the census. At its emptiest, it might not have provided Mary with the privacy she undoubtedly wanted. Palestinian inns were more like stockades than real buildings. A stout wall and a locked gate formed an enclosure. For the merchants who stopped at them, the important thing was that their merchandise and pack animals were secure from the ever-present bands of thieves.

But such an inn offered little in the way of comfort. A raised platform at one side of the enclosure was provided for the human patrons. At least it had a roof and it kept the milling animals from trampling on their sleeping owners. Wooden partitions divided the platform into stalls, but doors were unusual. It was hardly the place for an expectant mother.

Someone, perhaps the innkeeper himself, must have suggested to Joseph that they find shelter in an empty stable nearby. Paintings and Christmas crib scenes often show a shelter crudely constructed of wood, but more likely it was a cave.

Dark and miserable as such a place sounds to us, it may not have distressed Mary greatly. It was customary to make use of caves. In Palestinian hill towns houses often were, and still are, built up against the side of a mountain so that a natural cave, or one hollowed out of the soft limestone, could serve as an extra room. And there is no reason to think that Joseph and Mary's own house in Nazareth was any finer than their neighbors'. Life was simple in Palestine two thousand years ago. People slept on mats and ate sitting cross-legged on the floor. They cooked over tiny, movable ovens, or outside if the weather allowed, as the houses had no chimneys.

Luke says that "while they were there the time came for her to be delivered." Apparently Joseph had a few days to make the place livable, and we know he had the skills with which to do it.

And so, one night, the child was born, and Mary "wrapped him in swaddling cloths and laid him in a manger."

The swaddling cloths were the usual infant clothes of the day—a large, soft, square of cloth, rather like a modern receiving blanket, that was wrapped around the baby, and bands of firmer cloth that held the covering snugly in place. Extremely simple, they nevertheless were made with care and the bands often were embroidered. No doubt Mary had made hers in the little house in Nazareth and brought them with her to Bethlehem, knowing the child would be born before they returned home.

The manger, of course, was simply a feeding trough, set high enough for oxen or donkeys to feed comfortably. Perhaps it was made of wood; more likely it was formed from potter's clay and placed on a wooden support. Left over from when the cave had been used as a stable, it made a perfect crib for the newborn infant.

The gospels say that the news of the birth was first announced to shepherds. There were many around Bethlehem. The tiny village lay on the edge of a plain, a vast, uncultivated tract of semidesert land that was used only for pasturing flocks. The plain stretched twenty-five miles to the north, as many miles east and a far greater distance to the south. To the west Jerusalem, a great city only five or six miles away, provided a constant, ready market for foodstuffs of all sorts.

On the plain, groups of shepherds lived outdoors all year long, tending other people's flocks of sheep. The occupation of shepherd had once been an honored one among the Jews. After all, King David had been a shepherd on this same plain, and Bethlehem's one glory lay in being the "city of David."

But now shepherds often were looked down upon, even despised. Rough, ignorant men, they were poorly paid and usually wore ragged, dirty clothing. Moreover, they tended to ignore the regulations regarding the washing of hands and cooking utensils that made up an important part of Jewish law at the time. Prejudice against them was so strong that throughout Palestine the testimony of shepherds, like that of thieves and extortioners, was not admitted in a trial.

Nevertheless, the shepherds were the first to hear the joyful news of Christ's birth. Luke tells us that "an angel of the Lord appeared to them and the glory of the Lord shone around them and they were filled with fear." The angel must have seen this fear (more likely real terror), for his first words were "Be not afraid." One can sense a pause, while the panic-stricken men regained their senses. And then the angel continued with the words that are, after all, the ultimate message of Christmas,

> for behold, I bring you good news of a great joy which will come to all the people; for to you is born this day in the city of David a Savior, who is Christ the Lord. And this will be a sign for you: you will find a babe wrapped in swaddling cloths and lying in a manger.

Was there any great spiritual significance in the "sign" the angel mentioned, the swaddling cloths and the manger? Probably not. The word "sign" can have that sort of meaning in Old Testament writings, but it can also be used quite literally, and that seems to be the case here. The child is simply being identified. The swaddling cloths were customary, but the manger was highly unusual. It gave the shepherds a clue that they must search for this newborn infant not in the houses of Bethlehem, but in its stables.

The brief message ended as abruptly as it began, and Luke tells us that suddenly many, many angels were there, praising God, saying "Glory to God in the highest."

The shepherds, practical men, wasted no time in either speculation or contemplation. The gospel tells us that they "went with haste, and found Mary and Joseph, and the babe lying in a manger."

The crib scenes and the paintings always show the shepherds kneeling in homage, and no doubt they are correct; but after the first few moments of wonder and awe there must have been some conversation. The shepherds seem to have talked freely about their experience with Mary, with Joseph, with anyone they met. How Mary and Joseph responded we do not know. Luke merely says that "Mary kept all these things, pondering them in her heart."

Nor do we know how the villagers of Bethlehem accepted the excited declarations of the shepherds. Certainly they knew that the prophet had named their town as the birthplace of the coming Messiah, but mixed with a sense of destiny and hopefulness there might have been more than a touch of doubt and cynicism. Young men had come forward before claiming to be the Messiah. None had accomplished anything. The shepherds insisted they had heard messengers from heaven. The villagers saw only an apparently ordinary couple and a newborn baby. No doubt they came and looked and wondered, and then went about their business, remembering the words of the shepherds but not sure what to make of any of it.

Bethlehem has not changed a great deal in the last two thousand years, and shepherds still keep their flocks of sheep on the outskirts of town. Through oral tradition—often far more reliable than most people realize—the location of the birthplace has been handed down. St. Justin Martyr, who grew up in Palestine a hundred years after Christ, could write of the "neighboring cavern of Bethlehem" where Christ was born. A hundred years later, according to the Christian writer Origen, the cave with its manger where the infant had lain was known and pointed out even to pagans.

During the Roman persecutions of the early Christians, the emperor Hadrian deliberately ordered a grove sacred to the god Adonis planted around the site, but that only served to mark the area for succeeding generations. By 326 A.D. most of the Romans had become Christian, and the emperor Constantine began to build a basilica over and around the Grotto of the Nativity. The basilica still stands, one of the oldest churches in Christendom. Pilgrims can descend into the Grotto. A sanctuary light burns constantly. It is all very ornate. Present-day Christians might wish that the site had been left more the way it was, but it does seem probable that the traditional location is correct.

Luke describes the joy of the shepherds after they had seen the Christ Child, and then it is Matthew who continues the traditional Christmas story. He mentions the birth of Christ in one brief sentence—emphasizing again that it took place in Bethlehem—and proceeds to write about the wise men who came in search of the newborn king of the Jews, a journey begun because they had "seen his star in the East."

Who were these wise men? Writing in Greek, Matthew calls them "Magi." Originally the Magi were a priestly caste among the ancient Medes. Later they adopted Zoroastrianism, the religion of the ancient Persians. They were, at various times and places, known to be astrologers, priests, learned men and the counselors of kings. Matthew says that the Magi to whom he refers came "from the East." They were possibly from Persia or Babylonia, more probably from Nabatean Arabia, which extended as far north as Damascus in biblical times.

Tradition turned the wise men into the Three Kings and gave them names, but all that is legend. Nowhere does Matthew say that there were three. The number was probably arrived at because of the three gifts mentioned later in the account. Nor at any point does Matthew imply that they were kings. That tradition may have come from a misinterpretation of Psalm 71:10: "The kings of Tharsis and the islands shall offer presents; the kings of the Arabians and of Saba shall bring gifts." The names Gaspar, Melchior and Balthasar are first mentioned in an Armenian narrative written in the sixth century.

What was this star that had sent the Magi on their quest? Early Christians thought it was miraculous, and some scholars still support this point of view; but over the centuries numerous other possibilities have been brought forward. Artists and popular imagination have made the star a brilliant, breathtaking sight. Actually, it seems more probable that it did not attract any particular attention, as apparently few people noticed it or recognized its importance except the Magi.

Ordinary people in biblical times did not make a clear distinction among objects that they saw in the sky. Almost everything was commonly referred to as a star. Meteors, comets, novae and supernovae have all been suggested as the source of the new, unexpected light, but difficulties are encountered with each. Neither a single meteor nor a meteor shower lasts long enough to fit the description given by Matthew. Ancient records tell us that comets were visible in the spring of 5 B.C. and 4 B.C., but to the wise men, as to almost all early people, comets would have been omens of forthcoming disasters like famines, plagues and wars, not signs of the birth of a king.

A nova or supernova is, quite literally, an exploding star. It brightens quickly over several days and then very slowly dims over a period of weeks and months, and quite easily could fit the description given in the gospel. The astronomer Johannes Kepler first suggested this possibility in 1604. Unfortunately, though many ancient peoples kept detailed accounts of astronomical events, no certain record of a nova has been found for the probable time of Christ's birth.

If the Christmas star was indeed a natural phenomenon, a

conjunction of planets probably provides the best answer to the question. Such a conjunction occurs when two or more planets appear in nearly the same point in the sky. The planets are not really very close together. They just seem so because they are in the same direction in space when observed from the earth.

Jupiter and Saturn were in conjunction on May 27, 7 B.C. and again on October 5 and December 1 of that same year. To astrologers like the Magi, the planets were gods, and it was believed that their movements, if properly interpreted, could foretell coming events. Jupiter was thought to be the king of the gods, while Saturn was the special protector of the Jews. It was highly unusual for three conjunctions to happen in one year, and no doubt the Magi were watching intently to see what next might occur. Like many other people in the ancient world, they knew that the Jews were awaiting their Messiah. In February of 6 B.C., two months later, Mars, a more rapidly moving planet, joined Jupiter and Saturn. A conjunction of these three planets can take place only once every 805 years. Moreover, all three planets were in the constellation of Pisces, thought by astrologers to be the House of the Hebrews. To the Magi it would have been an overwhelming event, one that easily could have sent them off on their long journey.

The Magi apparently arrived in Jerusalem some months after the birth of Christ, and at once began to inquire of everyone, in high position or low, "Where is he who has been born king of the Jews?" The people of Jerusalem were startled and perhaps frightened. It was all well and good to dream secret dreams of a Messiah. At the moment the only king the Jews had was Herod, a brutal ruler contemptuously tolerated by the Romans. His palace was in Jerusalem. Its citizens were in his power. These foreigners were asking dangerous questions. Herod had already ordered the murders of his wife and two of his sons and numerous in-laws, as well as hundreds of lesser individuals who in some way had incurred his wrath. If his jealous rage were provoked again, who might be next?

The people's fears were well-grounded. When Herod heard the rumors sweeping the city, he at once sent for the chief priests and scribes and "inquired of them where the Christ was to be born." They answered truthfully. According to the prophecies, the promised ruler was to come from Bethlehem. Matthew briefly sums up Herod's next move. He summoned the wise men secretly and ascertained from them when the star had appeared; then he sent them to Bethlehem, saying, "Go and search diligently for the child, and when you have found him bring me word, that I too may come and worship him."

The Magi were probably too shrewd, too perceptive to believe Herod's fine words, but for the moment his motives did not concern them. They set out immediately for Bethlehem. Since they still saw the star, still felt that it was leading them onward, they must have left Jerusalem in the night. It was no great distance, and perhaps they were too eager to wait till morning.

Matthew says that "going into the house they saw the child with Mary his mother, and they fell down and worshiped him." The use of the word "house" has led some scholars to conclude that Joseph must have found better living quarters in town, but it also could be that he had continued improving the cave, changing its appearance so greatly that now it could be referred to as an ordinary dwelling.

Nor can we know for sure just what Matthew is implying when he says that the Magi "fell down and worshiped him." In their inquiries in Jerusalem the wise men had used this same word, "worship," but they spoke of seeking a king, not a god. It could imply adoration of the divine; it could suggest simply the homage due a great ruler. Belief in Christ's divinity came slowly, even for his disciples. We should not read more into the gospels of Luke and Matthew than is really there.

The treasures brought by the Magi, "gold and frankincense and myrrh," were typical of Eastern people, who would have thought it rude and discourteous to pay a visit to a superior without offering gifts. Frankincense was an aromatic resin obtained from certain trees growing in east Africa and Arabia. It was used as incense throughout the ancient world. Myrrh, also a resin, came from Arabia. Considered both rare and precious, it was used in perfumes, and for embalming.

Early Christian writers saw a great symbolism in the gifts. St. Irenaeus, writing in the second century, commented, "They offer myrrh to him who is to die, gold to him whose kingdom will not end, incense to the God of the Jews who now manifests himself to the Gentiles." But it is not likely that the Magi thought in those terms at all. The frankincense and myrrh probably were chosen because they were, like gold, extremely valuable, even in small, easily carried quantities.

The Magi must have stayed in Bethlehem for at least one night, for Matthew speaks of a dream in which they were warned not to return to Herod or to give him any information. By this time, no doubt, their own intuitions would have told them much the same thing.

Joseph, too, received a warning, and the family left Bethlehem hastily. Seeking a place where they would be safe from Herod's anger, they traveled south toward Egypt. Perhaps the gold came in handy on the long journey.

HYMN TO THE SUN

The people of Latium call you Sol
Because you alone are the crown of light
Held in honor after the Father.
They claim that your sacred head,
Brilliant with twelve rays,
Shines forth as many golden beams
As months of the year,
As sunlit hours of the day.
They say that you control four steeds with reins,
For you alone drive the chariot that nature furnishes.

Restraining the darkness,
You reveal the blue sky with your light,
So they call you Phoebus,
Foreteller of the future's secrets,
Or Lycaeus, because you break up the night's excesses.
The Nile worships you as Serapis,
Memphis adores you as Osiris,
Other cults revere you as Mithra, Dis, or savage Typhon.
You are also known as fair Attis,

and the gentle boy of the curved plow.
The parched Libyans pray to you as Ammon,
and Byblos, as Adon.
So the whole world calls upon you under different names.

MARTIANUS CAPELLA, fourth century A.D.,
translated by Florence Marie Gerdes, C.S.J.

The Ancient Festivals

THE WORLD was already old when Christ was born in Bethlehem. Civilization had followed civilization, and each had had its fears and its joys, its feasts and celebrations. Many were tied to the growing season, for farming provided the basis for mankind's first settled way of life.

Each year when the crops were gathered, the early farmers would rest a little, and rejoice that the harvest was in. But the end of the year was a frightening time, too. Around them the earth lay dying. If life did not return, if the growing season did not reappear, they knew that soon they, too, would starve and die.

In northern areas this barren time came in the winter. The trees were leafless, the ground was cold, and as the days grew shorter and shorter it seemed that even the sun had abandoned the world. In warmer climates it was not the cold that was feared, but drought. Lack of water, not lack of sun, ended the growing season and made the farmers and their families fearful and uneasy.

In Egypt life depended on water from the Nile River.

Crops could be planted only when the river rose, overflowed, and brought nourishing waters to the parched land.

At a very early date, probably more than five thousand years ago, the Egyptians began to watch the movements of the dog star Sirius, or Sothis—a brilliant object in the Egyptian sky. Its first appearance on the horizon each year coincided with the rising of the Nile, and the Egyptians believed that the star caused the waters to overflow. They declared Sothis to be the "creator of all green growing things," and eagerly watched for it in the half-light before the dawn. Counting the days between one appearance of the star and the next, the priests discovered that the year was made up of 365 days. They chose the star's annual day of reappearance in midsummer as the first day of the year.

Reassuring as it was to be able to predict the time of the river's overflow, a year of 365 days posed problems. At an even earlier period the Egyptians had had a lunar calendar based on the new moon's appearance every twenty-nine or thirty days. How could the old lunar calendar be reconciled with a year of 365 days? The Egyptians solved their problem by dividing the year into twelve months of thirty days each, and then adding on the extra five days at the end of the year. These days that belonged to no month, days that were spent awaiting the appearance of Sothis, became a festival time.

Wonder and laughter were a part of every Egyptian festival. The first days were spent mostly in preparation. On New Year's Eve the temples were rededicated. In the capital city the pharaoh himself performed the ceremonies, accompanied by the queen and numerous high priests. Fire was newly kindled and, as twilight deepened, throngs flocked to the temple courtyards to watch torchlight processions leave and begin to wind their way through the darkened streets. The next day, the first day of the New Year, was the Egyptians' most important holiday.

Both food and drink were abundant and people wore their finest clothes. Small gifts, perfume bottles or amulets inscribed *au ab nab* (all good luck), were exchanged between friends. Custom demanded that peasants and leaseholders present more sizable gifts to the lord whose land they worked, but these too were given in a holiday spirit. New Year's night was taken up with more torchlight processions, and only when exhaustion drove the crowds home was the festival officially ended.

In ancient Mesopotamia life was more uncertain. The land lay between the Tigris and Euphrates rivers; crops, and therefore survival, depended on the annual overflow from the rivers. But the Tigris and the Euphrates were not nearly as dependable as the Nile, nor as predictable. The people could not know exactly when the rivers would rise, nor how much water they would bring. They only knew that at certain times of the year the earth was parched and dry, that all growing things were dead, and that if water did not come again they would face eventual starvation.

These early Mesopotamians believed that the land was barren because Tammuz (later Marduk), the god of all growing things, was imprisoned in the underworld—held captive by the dragon Tiamat. It was the duty of the whole nation, and most especially the king, to help Tammuz fight his way back to earth so that the crops would grow again.

This battle became the theme of the Mesopotamian New Year's festival which, like the Egyptian holiday, began almost five thousand years ago. The celebration lasted for twelve days, and the mood was more somber than in Egypt, at least for the first days of the feast. Excitement, anticipation, but most of all fear, marked the beginnings of the ritual. The god Tammuz must be mourned. Even the king did penance, assuring the god that he had carried out his duties, that he had "not destroyed Babylon" (the great capital city). There was great commotion in the streets as crowds searched for the missing god and groups of men staged mock battles on his behalf. Bonfires were built, and in them were burned wooden effigies of the dragon Tiamat. Tension ran high. Tammuz must be found and freed; life must return to the land.

Finally, on the sixth day, the god triumphed. Rescued by his son, the god Nabu, he returned to earth victorious, and married Ishtar, the goddess of battles. The king, now impersonating the god, appeared amid wild rejoicing. Bands of costumed men roamed the city, forming torchlight processions at nightfall. For the next six days, gaily decorated wagons, filled with the statues of gods and goddesses, were paraded down the great avenues. More bonfires were built, and feasting and drinking went on all night. In the daylight hours friends visited each other and exchanged gifts. Finally, on the twelfth day, the statues of the gods and goddesses were returned to the temples. The people's fate had been decided for yet another year, and good had conquered evil. On the twelfth night one last and most uproarious feast ended the holiday season.

The ancient Babylonians had another festival, the *Sacaea*, which also was celebrated by the Persians. During the festival masters and slaves exchanged places. For a few days the slaves commanded, the masters obeyed. In each home one slave was chosen to be the head of the household, and everyone paid homage to him. In the palace a mock king ruled in place of the monarch. Little is known about the origins of the *Sacaea*, but the idea of a festival in which roles were reversed would persist for an unbelievably long time.

Egypt and Mesopotamia were the sites of the world's first great civilizations, but to the west other people were developing distinctive cultures of their own. As early as 2000 B.C. the people who would become the Greeks were pouring down into the Balkan peninsula and overcoming the earlier inhabitants.

Herders in their homelands in the north, they quickly copied the ways of their newly conquered neighbors and learned to grow grain, grapes and olives. They learned, too, of an already ancient god of the harvest—Cronus by name.

These earliest Greeks readily adopted other people's gods and goddesses. They thought of them as an immense family. Cronus became not only the patron of agriculture, but also the son of Uranus (Heaven) and Gaea (Earth); and the father of Zeus (god of the heavens), Hades (god of the underworld) and Poseidon (god of the sea).

The name Cronus was so similar to the Greek word *chronos*, meaning "time," that confusion was inevitable. Pictured as an old man, stooped and holding a scythe in his hands, Cronus comes down to us as the familiar figure of Father Time. His festival, the *Kronia*, was celebrated in midsummer, after the wheat had been harvested. Just as the people of Egypt and Mesopotamia had blessed the gods and rejoiced over the water that would bring a new crop, the Greeks gave thanks for grain already safely stored in the granaries.

The *Kronia* came at a time when there was little work to do in the fields. The slaves were idle, the masters relaxed. Perhaps because of this, the *Kronia* acquired the customs of the Babylonian and Persian *Sacaea*.

As civilization slowly spread westward along the shores of the Mediterranean Sea, other people in the north gazed down enviously upon sunny, grain-filled fields and prosperous vineyards. About 1000 B.C. wandering tribes called "Latins" entered the Italian peninsula. In time they built a village where seven hills stood beside the Tiber River. That village would grow and become the great city of Rome.

The early Romans were stern, upright, practical people, and their gods and their holidays were simple and uncomplicated. Saturn was the Roman god of agriculture. His festival, the

Saturnalia, came on December 17. It was a good time to have a feast. Food was plentiful, for early winter was butchering time. The grain, though long since harvested, had not yet begun to run low. Besides, the autumn sowing was completed and people had time to celebrate.

Over the centuries the Romans and their *Saturnalia* changed tremendously, but the festival always remained the merriest holiday of the Roman year.

The Romans were not particularly imaginative; their genius lay in conquest and in adapting and absorbing the customs of the people they conquered. They accepted the Greek gods and goddesses, combining them where possible with their own divinities. Saturn became identified with Cronus, and the *Saturnalia* soon began to resemble the Greek *Kronia.*

During *Saturnalia* slaves were given temporary freedom to do what they liked. Work was forgotten; they could drink, gamble, dress as free people and say what they pleased. Insults to the master that might at other times cost a slave's life were overlooked. At *Saturnalia* it was the slaves who reclined at table, eating the finest food, while the master was supposed to wait on them. Some Romans found this to be beneath their dignity. In many households the children were assigned the duty of serving the slaves.

The festival of *Saturnalia* which in the beginning had lasted only one day, was stretched to three days and later to seven. Only the first day of the feast had any religious significance. The rest of the time was spent in revelry.

The "anything-goes" spirit of the slave holiday soon spread to the rest of the population. Gambling, at least in public, was forbidden by Roman law, but an exception was made during *Saturnalia.* Any expression of anger or resentment was thought to be inappropriate during the celebration. No one was to be called to account for debt. The law courts were shut down;

punishment could wait. Schools were closed, to the delight of the children.

Gifts were exchanged, usually candles and little dolls called *sigillaria*. The candles were thought to be suitable, respectful gifts from persons of lower rank to persons of higher rank. The dolls were less formal gifts, token remembrances between friends, much like modern greeting cards. Once, no doubt, they had had some symbolic meaning, but that was soon forgotten. The little images—which in time included animals—were made of clay or other inexpensive materials, occasionally even of pastry. During the festival a special market, called like the dolls themselves the *sigillaria*, was opened for their sale. For the children, they were toys. For the adults, they were festive ornaments to be displayed around the house. Sometimes money gifts, called *sigillaricia* or *saturnalicia*, were substituted for the dolls.

The rich entertained at lavish private feasts, where a "king" was chosen by lot to preside over the revels. His commands, of course, were all in fun. Instead of the formal cumbersome toga, loose-fitting garments in bright colors were worn. The cry, "Ho, *Saturnalia*," was heard everywhere. Crowds jammed the streets, singing, dancing, eating, drinking, shouting and sometimes wearing outlandish costumes which often featured animal masks. Crude plays were performed. Torchlight processions wound through the city streets, much as in the earlier Mesopotamian holiday. The Romans, famous borrowers, were learning from the East.

As the *Saturnalia* became longer, it came closer to another Roman holiday, the *Kalends*, the Roman New Year. In earlier times the Roman year had begun on March 1, but gradually January 1 became the favored date. The change was officially recognized in 153 B.C.

The Romans strongly believed in fate. Omens were important to them and any undertaking needed a good start, an auspicious beginning. Certainly this was true of something so important as the new year. A kind of magic was involved. Not only would a good beginning foretell success, it could also cause good fortune. Such an attitude made a bountiful, exuberant New Year's festival inevitable.

The Roman New Year lasted from the evening of December 31 to January 4. The traditional greeting was "*Anno novo faustum felix tibi sit*" (May the New Year be happy and lucky for you). Gifts were exchanged to symbolize the good wishes. The earliest presents were green branches, called *strenae*. The name probably came from the goddess of health, Strenia, for the branches were thought to be symbols of life, health and vigor. In Mediterranean lands the favorites were branches of laurel (better known to us as the familiar bay leaf of the kitchen), olive and myrtle. As the Roman Empire and Roman customs spread to the north, the list came to include ivy, rosemary, holly and firs; and the simple branches were replaced by garlands and wreaths.

Soon *strenae* included many other things. Anything sweet would insure sweetness in the coming year; so dates, figs, honey, apples, pears, plums and little cakes all became popular. Nuts were favorite gifts for children; they served both as treats and as toys, for Roman boys used them as marbles. Anything golden promised wealth, so gilded dates and gilded nuts were happy choices for adults. Finally *strenae* became money, the simplest and most practical gift to both predict and cause good fortune. Any coin bearing the two-faced image of Janus, the god for whom the month January was named, was especially favored. The rich gave golden coins; the poor, gilded coppers or even gilded lead tokens. It was, after all, the thought that counted. Lamps, too, were popular gifts. They could be decorated with all sorts of symbols of good fortune—the laurel wreath, the winged figure of victory, the Janus coin, fruit and pots of honey—all worked into a harmonious design.

Among the wealthy the New Year gifts became much more than symbols. Gifts of money were thought suitable for persons of both higher rank and lower rank. The Emperor received gifts and so did the lowliest servant. Teachers were given gifts by their pupils, and all the persons who delivered goods to a household during the year expected to be remembered. For friends and relatives the gifts were more personal. Books, clothing, statues of gods and heroes, animals, birds, all kinds of food and even slaves were considered appropriate presents. Much emphasis was placed on selecting the right gift, something which would suit and flatter the recipient. Young boys and girls thought toys the finest present of all; children have kept that idea alive for twenty centuries.

Just as gifts could insure a lucky or wealthy new year, feasting could insure a bountiful one, and the lavishness of the Roman *Saturnalia* continued unabated into the *Kalends*. It was, as one Roman writer noted, a holiday for everyone but cooks and bakers. The carnival spirit continued also. Doorways were decorated with garlands and wreaths received as gifts, and houses were ablaze with candles and lamps. Troops of children paraded through the streets, singing and knocking on doors. If the householder answered, the children offered coins, expecting double in return. Most adults were happy to comply, for the exchange was supposed to increase the fortunes of both giver and receiver.

A few of the more sophisticated Romans objected to the effort and expense, but most people enjoyed the festive season. They looked forward to the winter holidays and would not have thought the year complete without them.

Despite the fine festivals, in many ways the Roman religion was impersonal and offered little emotional appeal. Further, it did not really provide any promise of individual immortality. It was almost inevitable, then, that as the Roman world expanded, various Eastern cults would become popular in Rome. The most important of these, at least for our story, was the religion of Mithra, the sun god.

Mithraism originated in Persia. Ahura Mazda was the ancient god of the Persians. The source of goodness and light, he was aided in his struggle against evil and darkness by Mithra, the god of battles, who was identified with the sun. After the fall of the Persian Empire in the fourth century B.C., the worship of Ahura Mazda was neglected and a new cult, centering on Mithra, grew up in its place.

Mithraism did not enter the Roman world until the first century B.C., and even then it was not immediately successful. It began to spread rapidly only after the beginning of the Christian era.

Mithraism was a man's religion; women were not allowed to enter its sacred ranks. Vigorous, simple and yet demanding, it had particular appeal for soldiers, and its first converts were found among the famed Roman legions. Military men could identify with a warrior god, a god whose duty it was to protect the world.

In 274 A.D. the emperor Aurelian proclaimed a new holiday. December 25 was to be celebrated as *natalis Solis Invictus* (the birthday of the unconquered sun). It was, according to the Roman calendar, the date of the winter solstice, one of the turning points of the year. The short days and long nights of early winter had ended. Now, with each passing twenty-four hours, the days would lengthen and the sun seem to grow stronger, until spring finally returned.

Aurelian, himself a former army officer, was undoubtedly a convert to Mithraism; but other, earlier, influences played a part in his decision to proclaim a new holiday. He came from the region around the Danube River, where solar worship was strong; his own mother had been a priestess of the sun. Now, heading a great empire, he hoped that devotion to the sun could help to unify the immense number of religious cults found within the Roman world. It seemed a reasonable idea, for almost all the people of the time did honor the sun—at least as one of many gods. At any rate, the new holiday came right in the middle of the Roman festive season, and it was a great success.

THE BOAR'S HEAD CAROL

The boar's head in hand bear I,
  Bedecked with bays and rosemary;
And I pray you, my masters, be merry,
  Quot estis in convivio:[1]

  Caput apri defero,
  Reddens laudes Domino.[2]

The boar's head, as I understand,
  Is the rarest dish in all this land,
Which thus bedecked with gay garland
  Let us *servire cantico:*[3]

Our steward hath provided this,
  In honor of the King of Bliss,
Which on this day to be served is,
  In *Reginensi atrio:*[4]

TRADITIONAL ENGLISH CAROL

---

[1] You who are at this feast
[2] The boar's head I bear, Giving praises to the Lord
[3] serve by singing
[4] the royal hall

Christmas Begins

It would be a good many years before December 25 became connected with Christianity. The earliest Christians avoided all pagan festivals, including the new "birthday of the unconquered sun." For that matter, they did not celebrate the birth of Christ, or any birthdays, thinking such things pagan and worldly.

If such an attitude seems strange, it must be remembered that the Christians lived always with the threat of persecution. The Roman government willingly tolerated the numerous pagan religions because their followers were willing to worship the emperor as the divine head of the state. When the Christians refused to join in the official worship, they were thought to be stubborn, disloyal men and women, and many were executed as a danger to the empire.

Faced with the constant possibility of a cruel death, the Christians had little interest in holidays. If there were to be any feast days, they preferred to commemorate the days on which martyrs had died rather than renounce their faith. Writing as late as the third century A.D., the Christian scholar Origen declared it wrong to celebrate the birthday of Christ "as though he were a king Pharaoh."

Despite the persecutions, Christianity spread rapidly throughout the Roman Empire, which now stretched across almost all of the known Western world. And gradually the prejudice against holidays decreased.

Epiphany (in Greek the word means "manifestation") began to be celebrated before Christmas was. In the east, in both Egypt and Greece, January 6 was the date of a pagan festival associated with rivers and water gods. Wishing to replace the pagan celebration with a Christian one, eastern Christians early in the fourth century instituted the Feast of the Epiphany. It began as a holy day commemorating the baptism of Christ in the Jordan River. To a lesser degree it also celebrated Christ's first miracle—the changing of water into wine at Cana—and the coming of the Magi.

These three events were linked together as examples of Christ's revealing, or manifesting, himself to the world as the Son of God. However, the older, pagan origin of the Epiphany feast shows through, almost two thousand years later. In Greek fishing communities, both in Europe and America, the traditional ceremonies still include the blessing of a sea or lake by a bishop. After his blessing, a crucifix is thrown into the waters. Young boys, all excellent swimmers, dive in and search the bottom for the cross, which is then returned in triumph.

An almanac written in the year 354 provides proof that Christians in Rome celebrated Christ's birth on December 25 at least as early as 336 A.D. A number of factors no doubt had influenced the change of attitude. The edict of Milan, issued by Emperor Constantine I in 313 A.D., had granted toleration to Christianity. Now Christians could relax and be more open about their faith and their feasts. Furthermore, the stalwart devotees of Mithra had provided the most stubborn resistance to Christianity. The Christians, suddenly finding themselves triumphant and perhaps a little startled with their success, hoped to placate the worshipers of the sun god. A festival occurring on the day most sacred to Mithra might provide a bridge over which the followers of the sun god could cross. After all, in St. John's gospel Christ was referred to as the Light of the World. And centuries earlier the prophet Malachi had even spoken of the promised Messiah as the Sun of Righteousness.

The trouble with building bridges, of course, is that traffic tends to go both ways. For the next century or two, Christian preachers found themselves having to remind their listeners firmly that it was Christ's birthday they were supposed to be celebrating, not Mithra's.

The church persevered, and what began as a holy day became a holy season. Gradually, as eastern Christians began to accept December 25 as the Feast of the Nativity, western Christians began to accept January 6 as the Feast of the Epiphany, which had become a holy day commemorating only the visit of the Magi. In 567 a great council or meeting of bishops at Tours, France, proclaimed the days between the two holidays to be a sacred and festive season, and so the twelve days of Christmas officially began. December 26 was chosen as the feast of St. Stephen, the first martyr, and December 28 was set aside to honor the Holy Innocents, the children of Bethlehem killed by Herod in his angry search for the Christ Child. A period of penance in the weeks preceding Christmas, called Advent, was added later in the sixth century.

The earliest truly Christian custom associated with Christmas seems to be that of the midnight mass. As early as the fifth century it was usual for the Pope in Rome to say three masses on Christmas: the first at midnight at the church of St. Mary Major, the second at dawn at the church of St. Anastasia and the third later in the day at St. Peter's basilica, which had been built in the previous century by the emperor Constantine I.

Solemn and reverent as the new customs were, they could not completely replace the old pagan ways. The feasting, the gifts, the boisterous good times of *Saturnalia* and the *Kalends* hung on and gradually blended with the Christian celebration.

But Christianity faced other problems as well. The Roman Empire was gone. It had crumbled rather than fallen, crushed by invading Germanic tribes. A great migration of peoples occurred in the fifth century. From their earlier homelands north of the Danube River and east of the Rhine, a horde of barbarian tribes pushed down upon a weakened empire. The Franks settled in what would become France, the Angles and the Saxons in Britain, the Lombards in Italy, the Visigoths in Spain. Now vast areas that had become Christian in Roman days were ruled again by heathen kings, and the church set out once more to convert the pagan conquerors.

Christmas, in those dark and troubled times, was considered a fine day for baptisms. Clovis, king of the Franks, was baptized along with three thousand of his men on Christmas Day in 496. One hundred years later St. Augustine chose Christmas as the day on which to baptize ten thousand Anglo-Saxons.

The people baptized in these mass ceremonies knew little about the faith they were supposed to be accepting, but sensible churchmen were willing to move slowly. Pope Gregory, in a message to Augustine, advised that since the Anglo-Saxons were

> wont to slay many oxen in sacrifices to demons, some solemnity should be put in place of this, so that . . . they may celebrate with religious feasting. Nor let them now sacrifice animals to the Devil, but to the praise of God kill animals for their own eating, and render thanks to the Giver of all abundance; so that while some outward joys are retained for them, they may more readily respond to inward joys.

> For from obdurate minds it is undoubtedly impossible to cut off everything at once, because he who strives to ascend to the highest place rises by degrees or steps and not by leaps.

The Pope was right. The conversion of the North would be a long and sometimes painful process. Pagan and Christian ideas coexisted for generations, and Christmas grew richer from the association.

The Germanic peoples had a great winter festival called Yule which lasted for twelve days and celebrated the end of the old year and the beginning of the new. As in early Rome, climate played an important part in the timing of the festival. In cold weather animals could no longer be turned out to graze, and both hay and grain were scarce. There was a very definite limit to the number of animals that a farmer could carry through the winter. The rest had to be killed. Slaughtering time was a natural time to sacrifice and to feast.

The origin of the word "Yule" is uncertain, as is the exact date of the festival. Many learned persons have tried to prove that it did or did not originally come at the time of the winter solstice, but perhaps it really does not matter. Christmas had already become a magnet, drawing many things to itself.

The wild pig was sacred to Frey, the Germanic god of peace and prosperity. Frey's companion was said to be a magical boar named Gullinbursti, with bristles of gold so brilliant they could light up the darkest night. Each year the largest boar that could be found in a village was set aside for the god Frey. On the eve of the Yule festival it was sacrificed to him in order to obtain good weather and good crops for the coming year. This *sonargoltr*, or atonement boar, was thought to be so holy that men would swear oaths and make vows with hands laid over the boar's bristles on the night it was to be killed.

The idea of the sacrifice of a pig to insure prosperity has been handed down in a number of ways. For centuries a boar's head was considered the high point of the Christmas feast in England. It was roasted, garnished with sprigs of rosemary and then served with an apple in its mouth. In earliest times wild boars were hunted for this purpose, but after the twelfth century they were extinct, and the heads of ordinary domesticated pigs had to be substituted. The custom lasted for a very long time. In the nineteenth century Queen Victoria and her family dined on the boar's head. Today the students at Oxford University continue to feast on, or at least applaud, the traditional fare.

In Sweden a pig's head, cured and then boiled, still is considered the finest and most attractive item on the Christmas table. Even modern cookbooks give detailed instructions for inserting the apple in the mouth without tearing the skin, and contain elaborate suggestions for decorating the head.

The old pagan ways show through even more clearly in the custom of the *julgalt*, a Yule boar made of dough, which the peasants of Sweden baked on Christmas Eve. A part of it was dried and kept till spring, when it was crumbled and fed to the plow horse and to the workers who would do the plowing, to insure a good crop. Today the Yule boar has all but vanished, but Christmas cookies and marzipan still are made in the shape of a pig.

Just as the pig was sacred to Frey, the horse was sacred to Woden, the god who gave victory in battle. In pagan times horses too were sacrificed at the Yule. This custom became attached to Christmas in two entirely different ways. In England horses were bled on December 26, St. Stephen's Day. Supposedly the taking of a small amount of blood from their veins insured the horses' health and soundness for the coming year. But before the blood was taken, they were raced till they were steaming—exactly as was done in older times with animals about to be sacrificed.

In many parts of Europe horses were, and still are, raced or blessed or given special feedings on the day after Christmas. Improbable legends developed to explain the practice. Stephen, a first-century Christian martyr whose death is described in the Acts of the Apostles, was made the patron of horses! Stories were told in which he became a missionary who traveled everywhere by means of five horses—two red, two white and one dappled. When one wearied he mounted another, and thus was able to cover great distances and preach to countless people. Eventually this seemed too farfetched even for the myth-makers, and a second Stephen was introduced. He was an eleventh century Swedish martyr, a Christian supposedly killed by pagans in the far north. His name, too, was linked to horses, and the customs continued to be observed on December 26.

The horse cult of barbarian Europe lingered on in yet another form, both in England and on the European continent. In many communities a fake horse pranced from door to door on the nights of the holiday season, half-frightening the children as it begged treats for its human companions. The beast was usually a carved wooden horse's head or a horse's skull attached to a pole and carried by one or several boys or young men who were concealed under sheets. Often its lower jaw was hinged so it could be made to snap menacingly. Sometimes, if a carved head was used, a lighted candle hidden inside produced fiery eyes and mouth. In Wales the creature was called the *Mari Llwyd*, while in England the most famous was "Old Hob," whose name shows a kinship with the hobbyhorse. In Germany, in Silesia and Pomerania, it was simply called the *Schimmel* (gray horse). Other similar figures turn up elsewhere in Europe, usually in small, rather isolated communities. In England the custom of the fake horse was called "Hodening," presumably a corruption of Wodening. Once, no doubt, it had been a sacrificial horse that was paraded from door to door.

The English Christmas horses roam no more, though the *Mari Llwyd* is rumored to appear occasionally in Wales, Unlikely as it seems, one such animal came to America and survived. "Old Buck" is the name given to the horse that has taken part in the holiday celebrations in the little village of Rodanthe, North Carolina, for as long as anyone can remember. Rodanthe is located on one of the islands of the outer banks near Cape Hatteras. Because of its isolation, early customs brought from England by its original settlers have continued there. "Old Buck" is identical both in construction and habits with the Christmas horses of old England, but in the 1950s one new note was added. On the horse's back rode a child, dressed as Santa Claus.

The custom of the wassail bowl, forerunner of the modern punch bowl, comes directly from the Anglo-Saxons. "*Waes-heil*" (which means, literally, "be well") was originally a toast, a pledge drunk between friends. The correct response was "*drinc-heil*" (drink well). In medieval England wassailing was an important part of the holiday season. In wealthy households a huge bowl, often of silver, was brought out not only on Christmas but also on New Year's and the Epiphany, and was filled with drink. Usually the beverage was "lamb's wool," consisting of heated ale, roasted crab apples, beaten eggs, sugar and spices. The poor would go from door to door, cup in hand, and beg in rhyme for a ladleful of the steaming brew. In time wassailing also came to mean caroling.

The word "wassailing" came to cover yet another curious holiday custom. In many parts of England, at some time during the holidays, farmers and their families or even a whole village would wassail the fruit trees, sprinkling them with cider, striking them with sticks and chanting some bit of rhyme bidding the trees to bear well in the coming year. The custom was practiced all over Europe until well into the nineteenth century, undoubtedly the remnant of some pre-Christian rite that was designed to insure a good crop.

But the best-known Christmas symbol handed down from the pagans of northern Europe is neither the boar nor the horse nor even the wassail bowl. It is the Yule log. Now usually associated with England, "bringing in the Yule log" was once a familiar and well-loved ritual throughout Europe. It was found not only in the old Germanic lands, but also in France, Spain and Italy, and especially throughout eastern Europe.

The basic rite was similar in every country, yet numerous regional variations occurred. The English version was perhaps the simplest. A great tree was found and cut on Christmas Eve. Size was all important, for the log must burn or at least smolder all through the twelve days of Christmas. A ponderous overturned oak was the first choice, preferably one with a twisted, massive root. Once found, it was dragged home amid much merriment, especially among the younger members of the family. As many people as possible grabbed a rope and helped to pull, for to do so was believed to bring good luck in the new year.

When placed on the hearth, the log could be lighted only with a brand from the last year's fire, and only by someone with scrupulously clean hands. When the holiday at last was over, remaining scraps of wood were put away carefully until the next year, when they would be needed to kindle the new fire. In the meantime it was believed that the wood scraps would protect the house against fire and lightning.

In some parts of England the Ashen Faggot was used in place of the log. It was composed of ash sticks bound together by nine ash or willow bands. Often the bands were named for the girls in the family; the one whose band was first to break would be the first to marry.

In southern France the log was called the *buche de Noël* (Christmas log). A fruit tree provided the preferred type of wood. The log was carried home by the children of the family in a single file beginning with the eldest and ending with the youngest. Three times around the kitchen, and then the log was laid on the hearth. The father or grandfather poured a glass of wine over it while saying, "Joy, joy, may God shower joy upon us, my dear children. Christmas brings all good things. God give us grace to see the New Year, and if we do not increase in numbers may we at all events not decrease." In chorus the children replied, "Joy, joy, joy!" and lifted the log onto the andirons. Then as the first flame leaped up, the father crossed himself, saying, "Burn the log, O fire," and the family sat down to the festive Great Supper of Christmas Eve.

As in England, the leftover pieces of wood were carefully saved, to protect the house not only from lightning but also from all sorts of other evils. It was believed that wood or ashes from the Christmas fire could cure cattle of various ailments, and that ashes strewn in the fields could save the wheat from mildew. Sometimes a piece of wood not scorched by the fire was used to make a wedge for a new plow, in the belief that such an implement would make the seed prosper.

In eastern Europe the ritual was more complicated and the log's magical powers even more emphasized. In Serbia, part of present-day Yugoslavia, the oaken log was cut down before sunrise on the day before Christmas. It was decorated with red silk, golden wire, leaves and flowers and brought into the house at dusk, surrounded by family members holding candles. Grain and sometimes wine were thrown on the log as it was carried over the threshold. Finally it was addressed in personal terms and placed on the fire by the oldest male member of the family, who then prayed for the blessing of God upon the household, its fields, cattle, sheep, bees and crops.

In remote villages in the Serbian highlands, fire irons, tables and stools were carefully removed to an obscure corner of the room before the log was brought in—an indication, perhaps, that the rites date from a time when such implements were unknown. After a simple supper, the night was spent in keeping the log burning brightly. Early the next morning a pig was roasted on the fire while the household anxiously awaited the arrival of a mysterious visitor called the *polaznik*—really a village boy chosen beforehand to play the role. When he came, the *polaznik* threw a handful of wheat on the family with the words, "Christ is born." All replied, "He is born indeed," and the mother threw wheat back at him. He then struck the burning log with a stick and wished "good luck, prosperity, progress and happiness" to the household and its beasts. It was generally agreed that there would be as many calves, lambs and piglets born in the springtime as sparks were struck from the log.

Despite the veneer of Christianity, such practices are obviously pagan, but their origin is long since lost. They cannot be Roman, for there is no mention of a Yule log in any Latin writing earlier than the sixth century A.D. The fact that the log is spoken to in personal terms hints at the tree worship that was once common among European peoples. But other, more sinister, clues can be found. In some parts of France chalk was used to draw a rude figure of a man on the log before it was burned. In Cornwall, England, the log was rarely called a log. Instead it was referred to as "the Mock," the phrase chillingly left unfinished. Viewed separately, neither of these practices might seem particularly sinister; taken together they suggest vague, dim memories of human sacrifice.

There are other possibilities for the origin of the Yule log.

Midsummer Night's Eve (later made Christian as the Feast of St. John the Baptist) was an important holiday for early Europeans. It marked the summer solstice—the longest day of the year, after which the days grow shorter and the nights longer as autumn and winter approach—and it was celebrated with huge bonfires. Cattle were driven through the edges of these fires, while people danced around them or jumped through them, in rites designed either to help the sun retain its strength or to help the crops grow. The Yule log may have been the winter counterpart of these fire festivals, turned into an indoor, family observance because of the cold and the danger that rain or snow might put out the precious fire if it was kindled outside.

Some scholars, emphasizing the Slavic, Eastern rite, have suggested that the custom of the Yule log stems from the fires of the New Year festival of ancient Mesopotamia, and that the log began as the wooden image of the dragon Tiamat. The idea may not be as farfetched as it sounds. Historians only recently have come to realize that ideas from the ancient East moved north along the Danube River as well as west to Rome. Those who favor this interpretation point out that fortune-telling and an emphasis on fate have always been an important part of the holiday observances of eastern Europe. Whether coincidental or not, these customs do bear a curious similarity to those of the Mesopotamian festival.

Whatever the origin, few if any Yule logs are lit today. In England the custom is chiefly remembered in song and story, and as a theme for Christmas cards. In France the *buche de Noël* has become a lavish chocolate cake, filled and rolled like a jelly roll, generously frosted to resemble a log, and trimmed with marzipan mushrooms. In this new and delectable form it rapidly is becoming popular in the United States, although here holly leaves and berries of frosting are the more usual decoration.

One other northern people added their ancient customs to Christmas. Long before the Romans or the Angles and the Saxons came to the British Isles, these lands were inhabited by the Celts. The Celtic god of the harvest was Daghda; he forever stirred a vast cauldron called Undry. It was filled with a porridge of cereal, fruit and meat, which symbolized all the good things of the earth. The Celts, in imitation of their god, served a similar dish at their great feasts. This mixture is the direct ancestor of all the plum puddings so greatly prized by the English. The concoction remained a porridge until well into the eighteenth century, when it finally was changed into a more solid pudding. The combination of meat and fruit, all but unknown in other countries of Europe, would later be fortified with the spices brought home by the Crusaders, and turned into mincemeat.

For hundreds of years in England, France and most especially in Ireland, bands of boys "hunted the wren" on the day following Christmas. When a wren was found it was killed and fastened to a mass of greenery atop a pole. Parading it from house to house, the boys would sing,

> The wren, the wren, the king of all the birds,
> St. Stephen's Day was caught in the furze;
> Although he is little, his family's great.
> I pray you, good landlady, give us a treat.

The oldest version of any custom is often to be found on an island because islands, by their very nature, are isolated, and change comes slowly in isolated areas. On the Isle of Man, in the Irish Sea between England and Ireland, an even stranger variation of this rite prevailed. On Man—which for centuries was thoroughly Celtic—the wren was hunted not on St. Stephen's Day, but very early on Christmas morning. After midnight mass a crowd would go to find a wren and kill it. Fastening it to a pole, they proceeded from house to house at daybreak, singing,

We hunted the wren for Robin the Bobbin,
We hunted the wren for Jack the Can,
We hunted the wren for Robin the Bobbin,
We hunted the wren for every one.

After collecting all the money they could they would carry the wren in procession to the churchyard. There, according to the nineteenth century antiquarian, William Walsh, the people would bury the wren "with the utmost solemnity, singing dirges over her in the Manx language which they called her knell," after which a circle dance was performed in the churchyard. Only then could Christmas begin.

The custom must have its roots in pre-Christian animal sacrifices, but its meaning has disappeared forever. So, very nearly, has the practice itself. It died out on its own in France in the seventeenth century. It was deliberately stamped out in England in the nineteenth century by the Society for the Protection of Animals. The Manx chant became a nursery rhyme, and today the custom survives only in a few remote communities in Ireland. Mercifully, the wren used now in Ireland is fake—sometimes merely a little bunch of feathers—and the whole rigmarole serves only as a pleasant pastime for children and as a way to raise money so that the young people of the village can have a holiday dance.

THE TWELVE DAYS OF CHRISTMAS

On the first day of Christmas my true love sent to me
A partridge in a pear tree.

On the second day of Christmas my true love sent to me
Two turtle doves
And a partridge in a pear tree.

On the third day of Christmas my true love sent to me
Three French hens
Two turtle doves
And a partridge in a pear tree.

On the fourth day of Christmas my true love sent to me
Four Colly birds . . . .

On the fifth day of Christmas my true love sent to me
Five gold rings . . . .

On the sixth day of Christmas my true love sent to me
Six geese a-laying . . . .

On the seventh day of Christmas my true love sent to me
Seven swans a-swimming . . . .

On the eighth day of Christmas my true love sent to me
Eight maids a-milking . . . .

On the ninth day of Christmas my true love sent to me
Nine drummers drumming . . . .

On the tenth day of Christmas my true love sent to me
Ten pipers piping . . . .

On the eleventh day of Christmas my true love sent to me
Eleven ladies dancing . . . .

On the twelfth day of Christmas my true love sent to me
Twelve lords a-leaping,
Eleven ladies dancing,
Ten pipers piping,
Nine drummers drumming,
Eight maids a-milking,
Seven swans a-swimming,
Six geese a-laying,
Five gold rings,
Four Colly birds,
Three French hens,
Two turtle doves,
And a partridge in a pear tree.

TRADITIONAL ENGLISH CAROL

The Joyful Holiday

GRADUALLY, over the centuries, the barbarian conquerors from the north merged with their formerly Roman subjects. Europe, and Christmas, became a blend of Celtic and German, Roman and Slav. New nations grew up, and new languages were formed.

When Latin was no longer the language of the people, the day celebrating the birth of Christ acquired new names. In Latin from the earliest times it had been called *Festum Nativitatis Domini Nostri Jesu Christi* (the Feast of the Nativity of Our Lord Jesus Christ) or, more simply, *Dies Natalis Domini* (the Birthday of the Lord). From the Latin, but possibly still echoing a final salute to Mithra, the sun god, came *Il Natale*, used in Italy; *La Navidad*, in Spain; *Natal*, in Portugal; and *Nadolig*, in Wales. The French *Noël* may stem from the same root, or it may have been derived from the Latin *novella*, meaning news —in this case the glad tidings of the gospel. In Germany the feast became known as *Weihnacht* (holy night), while the Scandinavian countries simply kept their old pagan *Jul*. The English word "Christmas," used as early as 1038, and the Dutch *Kermis* both originally meant "Christ's mass."

Among eastern Europeans—Romanians, Magyars, Bulgarians, Serbs, Russians, Lithuanians, Czechs and Poles—Christmas, Christmas songs and Christmas gifts are called variously *Kolind*, *Koleda*, *Kolenda*, *Koljada*, *Kolyada*, *Kaledos* and other names, all deriving from the Latin *Kalendae* (New Year's).

By the early Middle Ages the character of Christmas had been formed. It was a day both solemn and joyous, sacred and festive. Kings favored it as a day for coronations. Charlemagne was crowned Holy Roman Emperor on Christmas Day, 800 A.D. William the Conqueror chose Christmas of 1066 for his coronation as King of England. Later, after the brief success of the first Crusade, Baldwin of Edessa received the crown of the Latin Kingdom of Jerusalem on Christmas of 1100. Even in legend Christmas was full of good omens, for it was on this day that Arthur was said to have withdrawn the sword Excalibur from its resting place, proving himself to be the rightful king of Britain.

When medieval kings celebrated, the feasting was prodigious. Henry III of England required "six hundred fat oxen" for the Christmas feast of 1252, which was also the wedding banquet for his daughter's marriage to the king of Scotland. Great barrels of ale and wine washed down the meat, which was accompanied by a variety of side dishes. Some medieval delicacies with names like dellegrout, maupigyrum and karumpie have vanished forever. The ingredients can only be guessed at. Others, like pies made of carps' tongues, and peacocks roasted and then served with all the feathers carefully back in place, would hold scant appeal for most modern tastes.

Sometimes the royal Christmas season was taken up with affairs of state, but if no pressing business was at hand, a tournament often was arranged, with games that imitated warfare. Knights would come, many from other countries, accompanied by heralds, minstrels, pages, squires and the elegant noblewomen whose colors the knights would wear in the contests. The sport was dangerous; often men were wounded and occasionally they were killed, but nothing dampened the enthusiasm of the monarch or the participants.

Roman ways proved surprisingly persistent in this new world of the Middle Ages. Customs which the earliest Christians had firmly denounced were finally accepted and, quite literally, blessed.

Candles were probably the first of the old Roman symbols to become accepted in the Christian celebration. They were, after all, a natural sign of joy and hope during the gloomy days and long nights of early winter. Moreover, they could easily be interpreted as a symbol of Christ, the Light of the World. A candle in the window was a sign of welcome to travelers; soon it was seen as a welcome to the Christ Child, for he, too, had once been in need of shelter.

In many of the countries of Europe, a large Christmas candle was an important part of the holiday ritual in even the poorest household. It was lighted with ceremony, usually on Christmas Eve, often by the oldest member of the family. In some places it was allowed to burn all night, and only extinguished at dawn. In others it had to burn till the very end of Christmas Day, or be relit each night till the twelve days were ended.

The distinctively Roman notion that candles were a suitable gift for someone of superior rank lasted unchanged for centuries in England. Writing in 1841, an English antiquarian noted that "the poor were wont to present the rich with wax tapers, and yule candles are still given by merchants to their customers." At one time children in the village schools in Lancashire, England, were expected to bring candles for their teacher before the school closed for the Christmas holidays.

The custom of exchanging holiday gifts also spread to many

countries. In France gifts are given on New Year's, rather than Christmas. The gifts were, and still are, called *étrennes*, a word taken directly from the Latin *strenae*, the gifts of the Roman New Year. The Spanish word *estrenas* is also derived directly from the Latin, though sometime in the Middle Ages the gift-giving day was changed from New Year's to January 6, when the feast of the Three Kings was celebrated. In Germany until the nineteenth century a typical present for a child was an apple with a coin stuck in it, which combined two of the favorite gifts of Roman days.

England clung to two traditions immediately recognizable as Roman. All through the Middle Ages the kings of England demanded sizable holiday "gifts" from their subjects, just as the emperors had in pagan days. And in England, even today, servants and those who make deliveries for shopkeepers often are given gifts, usually of money, on Boxing Day, December 26. Traditionally the money was collected in little clay boxes almost identical with those used in Rome for the same purpose two thousand years earlier.

Tenacious as the gift-giving customs were, presents in the Middle Ages were mostly exchanged among the rich, or given by the rich to the poor. Except for simple treats for the children, a poor family—and there were very few who were neither rich nor poor—had to look elsewhere for its merriment.

One form of holiday merrymaking available to all was mumming, also called guising. The word "guising" is related to the more familiar "disguise"; the origin of the word "mumming" is uncertain. But there is no mistaking the source of the custom—*Saturnalia* survived in yet another form. Throngs of merrymakers crowded the streets, dressed in every conceivable costume. Masks shaped like animal heads were favored, but so was the idea of men dressing up in women's clothes. Singing, dancing, begging were all part of mumming. In smaller villages every house was called on, and the mummers were given treats of one sort or another. The custom was widespread throughout the Middle Ages. Prevalent in England and France, it also was practiced enthusiastically in much of southern and eastern Europe.

Both church and state disliked mumming. In the carnival spirit excesses were inevitable, and the costumes—which made identification all but impossible—were to some an invitation to crime. But for centuries mumming was impossible to suppress. Finally, in the south of Europe, the practice drifted away from Christmas and instead became part of the pre-Lenten carnival season. In eastern Europe the wild mummers changed into Star Boys—troops of costumed children carrying lighted stars and caroling from house to house. Mumming survives today in a few parts of Germany, notably in Bavaria. In the Berchtesgaden area of southern Germany, it has been combined with the custom of "shooting in" both Christmas and New Year's. Societies of marksmen wearing traditional uniforms welcome the holidays at midnight by firing round after round from antique rifles.

In England crude plays sometimes had been performed by the mummers, and certain stock characters, of whom St. George was most important, were introduced. In almost every version two antagonists fought to the death, and then the hero was revived. The resemblance to the old idea of a god of vegetation who dies at the end of the year only to come to life with the new growing season is unmistakable.

Gradually the informal mumming ceased, and only the plays, in an ever more structured form, survived. They are still performed in a few English towns. In other places the mumming turned into simple begging, especially by poor children. A little ditty, now popular as a children's Christmas song, is a remnant:

Christmas is coming, the goose is getting fat,
Please put a penny in the old man's hat.
If you haven't got a penny, a ha'penny will do,
If you haven't got a ha'penny, God bless you!

English mumming lasted long enough to come to America. The plays were popular in many communities in the eighteenth and early nineteenth centuries. But the figure of St. George, after the Revolution, was no longer sufficiently patriotic. In most communities he turned into George Washington! Mumming itself, in the old medieval manner, survives today in only a few out-of-the-way places. Folklore enthusiasts have discovered it in Newfoundland. And in Rodanthe, North Carolina, it still provides a natural accompaniment for the parades with the horse "Old Buck." In a handful of remote communities in the American South, men for generations have ridden around on New Year's Eve, "shooting in" the New Year.

But it is in the large and modern city of Philadelphia that mumming has made its strongest stand. It came with the English settlers, who brought their comic plays, and with the Swedes, the earliest settlers along the Delaware River, who brought their own tradition of roaming bands of masqueraders. By the nineteenth century little was left of either custom, except that in the southern part of the city bands of merrymakers, dressed in fantastic costumes, went about on New Year's Eve, shooting off firearms and making as much noise as possible.

Many people wanted to keep the tradition alive. Gradually clubs were formed whose chief business was to prepare for the mumming each year. In 1901 the Philadelphia city government (which had formerly disapproved of mumming because of the mischief that went with it) issued permits for a parade, and three thousand masqueraders marched down Broad Street on New Year's Day. The parade has continued to grow and today it is a Philadelphia institution, quite similar in many ways to the New Orleans Mardi Gras parades, and springing from the same ancient roots.

Besides mumming, Christmas in the Middle Ages had other diversions. In England gambling was generally forbidden to apprentices and others; but here, too, the influence of *Saturnalia* shone through. Dice and playing cards were an important part of the holiday season. Riddles, sometimes ribald, added to the merriment.

In the great houses, in the king's court and even in the early colleges, a Lord of Misrule directed the holiday revels. He was a direct descendant of the king of *Saturnalia*, a master of ceremonies whose every command must be obeyed. But, in time, his real job became to arrange for elaborate pageants called masques, and entertainments of all sorts; and to make sure that everyone enjoyed every one of the twelve days of the festive season.

Within the church the lower clergy had the same sort of celebration, called the Feast of Fools. In the Middle Ages deacons, subdeacons and clerks were for the most part poor men, poorly educated, and often with little or no real calling for the vocation they had undertaken. But at Christmas the church could be theirs, for one day at least. One of their number was chosen to lead the festivities. He was given the title of archbishop, cardinal or even Pope, dressed in elaborate vestments, and seated on the bishop's throne. His commands alone would be obeyed—commands that were never very dignified, and sometimes downright scandalous.

It was the old topsy-turvy world of *Saturnalia*, *Kronia* and *Sacaea* spilling over into the church itself. Eating, drinking, playing at dice and wearing masks were all part of the festivities. In France a donkey was paraded through the church. Once, perhaps, it had represented the donkey of the Nativity scene, but that too had been forgotten. The mock hymn that greeted it ran:

From Oriental country came
A lordly ass of highest fame,
So beautiful, so strong and trim,
No burden was too great for him.
  Hail, Sir Donkey, hail.

Many, perhaps most, people viewed the Feast of Fools as blasphemous, but the bishops, popes and kings had to struggle for several hundred years before it was entirely suppressed.

Closely connected, but far more attractive, was the practice of electing a boy bishop to serve on December 28, Holy Innocents' Day, which had become the official feast of students and choirboys. Arrayed in the robes of a bishop, the boy sang Vespers, gave a sermon and sometimes questioned his fellow students on the catechism. The custom lasted until the sixteenth century when the Reformation led to the establishment of new Protestant churches in many parts of Europe and in England.

The English King Henry VIII forbade the custom, only to have it deliberately reinstated by his eldest daughter, Mary, when she succeeded him to the throne. Mary, loyal to the old ways, brought Catholicism back to England and wanted everything to be as it had been before her father's break with Rome.

In December of 1555 she was entertained by the child bishop of St. Paul's Church, London, who, with his company, sang before the queen on Holy Innocents' Day. He was the last of his kind, for with Queen Mary's death the old custom vanished, never to return. On the Continent the practice was blended with St. Nicholas's Day, and then gradually forgotten.

By the thirteenth century it was obvious that the Christian aspect of Christmas was being lost in a welter of pagan remnants that sometimes seemed nothing more than superstition and carousing. This particularly troubled Francis of Assisi, a young Italian nobleman who abandoned a comfortable worldly life and founded the Franciscans, a religious order dedicated to serving the poor.

Francis, a truly gentle man burning with the love of God, wanted to inspire in others the devotion he felt toward the Infant Jesus. In December 1223, about two weeks before Christmas, he called on a good friend named Giovanni Velitta and said to him,

> If you desire that we should celebrate this year's Christmas together at Greccio, go quickly and prepare what I tell you; for I want to enact the memory of the Infant who was born at Bethlehem, and how He was deprived of all the comforts babies enjoy; how He was bedded in the manger on hay, between an ass and an ox. For once I want to see all this with my own eyes.

Velitta and his friends did their best. By Christmas Eve all was ready. Franciscan friars came from miles round. Francis's friend and biographer, Thomas of Celano, continues:

> The men and women of the neighborhood, as best they could, prepared candles and torches to brighten the night. Finally the Saint of God arrived, found everything prepared, saw it, and rejoiced. The crib was made ready, hay was brought, the ox and ass were led to the spot . . . . Greccio became a new Bethlehem. The night was made radiant like the day, filling men and animals with joy. The crowds drew near and rejoiced in the novelty of the celebration. Their voices resounded from the woods, and the rocky cliff echoed the jubilant outburst. As they sang in praise of God the whole night rang with exultation.

Francis stood before the crib, overcome with devotion and wondrous joy, and a solemn mass was sung.

The ox and the ass, though not mentioned by Luke in the

gospel, were already an old tradition. As early as the fourth century they had been represented in pictures of the Nativity, probably because of the words in Isaiah 1:3, "The ox knoweth his owner, and the ass his master's crib: but Israel hath not known me and my people hath not understood."

The dramatization of the scene in the stable in Bethlehem that Francis had requested inspired countless others. At first only live presentations were attempted. Later miniature figures were used, generally carved of wood but occasionally made from other materials. The Holy Family, the shepherds, the wise men were made with loving care. The custom spread rapidly from country to country. In France the crib scene was called a *crêche,* a name frequently adopted in English; in Italy, a *presepio;* in Germany, a *Weihnachtskrippe;* in Spain, a *nacimiento.*

The earliest cribs with figurines probably were made in Bavaria and in the Tyrol, where wood carving was already an art, but the custom soon found its way to central and southern Italy. It was brought to its artistic height in Naples during the eighteenth century. Here every leading family, including the king and queen, vied to have the most beautiful and elaborate presentation on display at holiday open houses. Wealth could command talent. Noted sculptors made sophisticated figurines with heads and shoulders delicately modeled in terra-cotta, arms and legs of finely carved wood, and bodies made of fiber and wire for pliability. Costumes were of the finest materials and often trimmed with jewels. To the customary Holy Family, shepherds and wise men were added numerous other figures—animals, townspeople, angels without number, and often a miscellaneous host of people from every land, representing all who would have come to Bethlehem if only they had known.

Today such elaborate sets are in museums, but the *presepio* remains an important part of Christmas in most Italian homes.

Bethlehem, in the scenes, closely resembles an Italian village in the hills. A delight in miniaturization has produced turning windmills, sprinkling fountains and springs that flow into streams and move waterwheels.

The crib scene was brought to America by the Moravians, a small Protestant group from Germany that founded the town of Bethlehem, Pennsylvania, on Christmas Eve, 1741. To them it was a *putz* (from the German word *putzen*, which means "to decorate"). Like the Italian *presepio*, the Moravian *putz* was constructed with deep devotion, and became larger and more elaborate as the years passed. Today a *putz* may include dozens or sometimes hundreds of figures, elaborate landscaping, waterfalls, houses and bridges, castles and sawmills—the whole lit up by miniature electric lights.

The new spirit of devotion influenced Christmas in yet another way. Latin hymns had been sung in honor of the Nativity almost from the first years of the celebration, but they were sternly theological with little or no emotional appeal. The early Franciscans wanted to humanize Christianity, give it warmth and tenderness. There was no better place to start than with the Child at Bethlehem.

Jacopone da Todi was the first to write the new songs. Jacopone was born into a wealthy family in Italy and became a successful young lawyer. He married, only to lose his beautiful girl-wife in a tragic accident a year later. Giving up his worldly life, he joined the Franciscans and became a poet—a man who has been described as producing "the first real outburst of Christmas joy in a popular tongue." To Jacopone the Christ Child was "our sweet little brother." Mary, in his songs, "rocked and hushed her boy" while "little angels" sang, "reverent, timid and shy round the little Baby Prince." It was a very different view of Christmas, and one the common people loved.

The Franciscans sang Jacopone's verses as they walked from village to village, preaching and teaching. And soon all of Italy was singing the new hymns of joy.

Much the same thing was happening in Germany, which in the fourteenth century was undergoing a religious revival inspired by the Dominicans, a new religious order that had been founded by St. Dominic. Soon every country in Europe had joyful Christmas songs, sung in the language of the people. In France they were called *noëls*; in Germany, *Weihnachtslied*; and in England, carols. The English carol began as a dance song, and there once were springtime carols too, but few of these have survived. The new songs were simple, gay and spontaneous. Some told a story, others were set in the form of a dialogue. Most had a religious theme; a few were frankly secular. But the message was always "Rejoice!"

Great changes had occurred in Europe in the thirteenth and fourteenth centuries, but even more important milestones were reached in the period that followed. The Renaissance, a rebirth or reawakening of learning after the isolation of the Middle Ages, began in Italy. Scholars turned back to the writings of ancient Greece and Rome, and a new movement called Humanism arose. The Humanists, as their name implied, took a deep interest in human beings and in the things of this world.

Their ideas, startling to a society that for centuries had tried to emphasize only the spiritual side of life, influenced artists as well as scholars. Painting and sculpture—though often remaining religious in theme—became more realistic, more natural, portraying the earthly beauty to be found in this world.

Nowhere is this tendency more noticeable than in the Renaissance paintings of the birth of Christ, the Nativity scenes. Almost all the great artists of the Italian Renaissance painted the Madonna (old Italian for "My Lady") and Child, and in doing so left a visual legacy that has never been surpassed.

In most early paintings of the Virgin and Child, dating from the fourth to the thirteenth centuries, Mary seems stern, almost forbidding, as she holds up the Divine Infant for adoration. Not so in the Renaissance! In these new portraits of Mary, sweetness, tenderness and maternal love radiate from her image.

The idea of a painting that would include both Mary and her mother, St. Anne, interested Leonardo da Vinci, one of the greatest of the Renaissance artists, over a period of years. One early version is a charcoal drawing done on brown paper, made around 1499 as a preliminary sketch for a painting. A little larger than life-size, it shows Mary, her mother, the infant Christ Child and his cousin, John the Baptist. Mary gazes fondly at her child, who raises his hand to bless young John, while St. Anne's attention is focused solely on her daughter.

Leonardo, restless and rarely satisifed with his work, set the drawing aside as not worthy of completion. Fortunately it was not destroyed, for viewers over the centuries have marveled at the sense of extraordinary beauty and affection it conveys. Today it hangs in the National Gallery in London, the only picture honored by being displayed alone in a room.

Some years later Leonardo returned to the same theme and produced the painting known as *The Virgin and Child with St. Anne*. In this later work St. Anne bears a curious resemblance to Leonardo's earlier *Mona Lisa*. As in the earlier drawing, she gazes calmly at her daughter. John the Baptist is no longer present. Mary bends sharply forward to restrain her son, who wishes to play with a young lamb. Critics have suggested that Leonardo was combining a deeply religious theme with a purely human emotion. The mother of Jesus, torn by indecision, reaches toward him, trying to hold him back from his destiny—the crucifixion, here symbolized by the sacrificial lamb.

Michelangelo Buonarroti, Leonardo's contemporary,

painted one truly magnificent representation of *The Holy Family*. The painting was commissioned by Angelo Strozzi, a wealthy nobleman from Florence, Italy, who wanted to present it as a gift to his bride at their forthcoming wedding. Michelangelo, who had recently completed two intensely spiritual Madonnas, each done in marble relief, wanted this painting of the family to be just as completely human. Mary and Joseph would be strong, sturdy people; the child, vigorous and bursting with health. Choosing peasants from the surrounding countryside for his models, he created an affectionate family seated informally on the ground. Strozzi was unhappy with the painting and threatened to refuse payment, but his bride-to-be, Maddalena, insisted that she have it. No other gift would do. Michelangelo doubled his original price, and Strozzi reluctantly agreed to pay. Today the painting hangs in the Uffizi Gallery in Florence.

Raphael Sanzio, born a few years after Michelangelo, had a tragically short career; he died when he was thirty-seven. But in that time he completed more than forty paintings of the Virgin. Probably the best known are the *Madonna of the Chair* and the *Sistine Madonna*. The former is easily recognized by its distinctive circular form. Mary is seated on a low chair and holds the child on her knee, encircling him with her arms. The infant Jesus nestles close, while his cousin John gazes toward him, hands clasped around a reed cross which symbolizes the child's future.

In the *Sistine Madonna* Raphael turned from earthly warmth and affection to draw back, quite literally, the curtains and peer into heaven itself. Mary walks on clouds, carrying the Christ Child toward the viewer. Two cherubic angels gaze upward, while St. Barbara and St. Sixtus kneel in worshipful poses.

Titian, another great artist of the Renaissance, painted a

number of Madonnas during the course of his long, productive life. Most charming, perhaps, is his *Madonna with the Rabbit*, named for the pet with which Mary seems to be amusing her child. In the painting St. Catherine leans toward the Virgin as she holds the infant Christ. The child looks half-merrily, half-shyly at the rabbit, fascinated but almost fearful.

At the time the scene was painted, Titian had young children of his own. His wife, Cecilia, probably posed for the figure of the Madonna. He sought to show a happy young mother delighting in her child, and he succeeded.

Antonio Allegri, born in Correggio, Italy, usually is known by the name of his birthplace, the little town in which he spent his whole life. In his paintings Correggio excelled in contrasting light with dark shadow and, like Titian, gave his Madonnas a very natural and human kind of beauty. Correggio's *Night*, usually called *The Holy Night*, is one of the most famous portrayals of the Nativity scene. A radiant glow centers on the Christ Child, illuminating the face of Mary and, to a lesser extent, the faces of the shepherds and the hovering angels. The rest of the painting is as dark and somber as its title would indicate.

Each generation of artists has interpreted the scene in the stable at Bethlehem in its own way, which is as it should be. Yet countless thousands of people continue to visualize the first Christmas as it was portrayed by the masters of the fifteenth and sixteenth centuries, and the Renaissance Madonnas have become a very real part of the holiday tradition.

ABOVE: St. Lucia and a dark helper bring gifts on Christmas Eve in a nineteenth century German drawing *(Courtesy of General Research and Humanities Division, The New York Public Library)*. LEFT: St. Nicholas and his companion, Black Peter, in a nineteenth century Dutch painting by J. Schenkman *(Courtesy of The New-York Historical Society, New York City)*. RIGHT: Old Father Christmas with a wassail bowl, from an engraving by Robert Seymour, 1837 *(Culver Pictures)*.

Bringing in the Yule log in England, from a drawing by H. M. Paget (*The Bettmann Archive*).

The Lord of Misrule, a nineteenth century engraving (*Culver Pictures*).

Costumed mummers on Christmas Eve, an engraving by Alfred Crowquill, 1872 *(The Bettmann Archive)*.

LEFT: Queen Victoria, Prince Albert and their children celebrate Christmas at Windsor Castle, from *The Illustrated London News*, 1848 *(Courtesy of General Research and Humanities Division, The New York Public Library)*. RIGHT: Bringing in the boar's head at a nineteenth century Christmas feast, Queen's College, Oxford *(The Bettmann Archive)*. BELOW: In Norway, bundles of wheat or oats were mounted on poles at Christmas to chase evil spirits from the house *(The Bettmann Archive)*.

ABOVE: The first Christmas card, 1843, designed by J. C. Horsley *(Victoria and Albert Museum)*. RIGHT: *Presepio* figures made in Naples in the eighteenth century decorate the Christmas tree at The Metropolitan Museum of Art, New York City *(The Metropolitan Museum of Art, Gift of Loretta Hines Howard, 1964)*. BELOW: Thomas Nast's first published drawing of Santa Claus, from *Christmas Poems*, 1863-64 *(Culver Pictures)*.

AND IPHICLES

UP ON THE HOUSETOP

Up on the housetop the reindeer pause,
Out jumps good old Santa Claus;
Down through the chimney with lots of toys,
All for the little ones, Christmas joys.

Ho, ho, ho! who wouldn't go!
Ho, ho, ho! who wouldn't go!
Up on the housetop click, click, click,
Down through the chimney with good Saint Nick.

First, comes the stocking of little Nell;
Oh, dear Santa, fill it well;
Give her a dollie that laughs and cries
One that will open and shut her eyes.

Ho, ho, ho! who woudn't go!
Ho, ho, ho! who woudn't go!
Up on the housetop click, click, click,
Down through the chimney with good Saint Nick.

Next, comes the stocking of little Will;
Oh, just see what a glorious fill!

Here is a hammer and lots of tacks,
Also a ball and a whip that cracks.

Ho, ho, ho! who wouldn't go!
Ho, ho, ho! who wouldn't go!
Up on the housetop click, click, click,
Down through the chimney with good Saint Nick.

BENJAMIN HANDBY, 1864

The Gift-Bringers

OUR ROOTS go deep into the cold, dark forests of northern Germany. Our English language began there. Four of our days of the week are named for the pagan gods of the north: Tiw, the god of war; Woden; mighty Thor; and Friga, gentle mother goddess in the sky.

Fire was particularly important to the peoples of northern Europe. The hearth had its own goddess, Berchta (or Perchta or Hertha or Hulda or Freke, for Germanic goddesses often had a half-dozen different names). Berchta was often associated with children. Occasionally she was described as a "white lady," bright, shining, beautiful.

In this role Berchta lives on in the Lucia Day celebrations of Sweden. December 13 in the church calendar is the Feast of St. Lucia. The real Lucy or Lucia was a Roman Christian who died for her faith early in the fourth century during the persecutions of the emperor Diocletian. But the name means light, and Lucy's feast day came at the time of the longest nights of the year. Inevitably the saint's day celebration became mixed with far older pagan customs, and Lucy took on Berchta's role.

Traditionally, in Sweden, Lucy was represented by the

oldest daughter of the family. Before dawn she dressed in white and cautiously placed on her head a crown of lighted candles. Thus arrayed, she went to her parents' bedside and offered them steaming cups of coffee and special saffron buns called *Lussekatter* (Lucy Cats).

By the nineteenth century the custom was dwindling and all but unknown in most parts of Sweden. Then a revival took place. Lucia Day became a Swedish national holiday, the opening of the Christmas season. Young people loved the candles, the costumes, the excitement. Today Lucias appear throughout Sweden on December 13. Even in hotel rooms startled guests find themselves awakened by carolers and served the traditional breakfast in bed.

Swedish-Americans have kept up the custom even more enthusiastically, though in this country the early morning breakfast service often is dropped in favor of an evening procession. On Lucia Day a Lucia Bride is crowned in a ceremony not unlike a beauty contest, and the runners-up become her court.

But only rarely was Berchta, the old hearth goddess, thought of as a radiant goddess of light. More often she was portrayed as a witch—an ugly old woman with a long nose, big teeth and bristling, thick-matted hair. Her feet were huge, the better to trample wicked, disobedient children.

For all her frightful appearance, Berchta was thought to have a kindly heart, at least part of the time. Troubled by the Christian missionaries' declaration that only the baptized could enter heaven, German mothers entrusted the souls of their unbaptized infants to Berchta's care. In the ninth century Christianity rested lightly on its recent German converts. If the new god would not accept the unchristened, surely the old goddess would care for them.

Legend maintained that Berchta kept close watch over the German households of long ago. It was she who made sure young girls learned to spin. Sometimes the lazy found empty spools left by the goddess, who threw them in an open window and expected to find them full of new thread when she returned.

Accompanied by a band of elves and sprites, Berchta rode through the land in the long dark nights at the end of the year. Sometimes she drove a wagon and sometimes, like Woden, she rode a great pale-colored horse across the sky. Each home was visited in the twelve days of the pagan Yule. The visit was half-feared, half-welcomed. A meal, usually fish and dumplings, had to be left for Berchta in case she was hungry, and a sheaf of oats for her steed. If all was in order, she pronounced her blessing. If things were not to her liking, she left a curse instead. Good was rewarded and laziness punished.

Berchta survives in unlikely places, far from her original home in Germany. Carried south by wandering Germanic tribes in the fifth century, she lives on in Italy. She gained a Christian name, Befana, from *Epifania* (the Feast of the Epiphany), but the identity is unmistakable.

Italian children believe that Befana is a tiny, misshapen old woman, dark and ugly and dressed in black. Riding a broomstick, she goes from house to house on the eve of the Epiphany, January 6. Sometimes she uses her broomstick to slide down the chimney, sometimes she comes in through an open window. Good children find gifts; bad children find lumps of coal or bags of ashes. Sometimes it is said that the really wicked are carried off by Befana.

Often, when pagan customs blend with Christian feasts, fanciful legends arise to provide Christian explanations for the old practices. So it is with Befana. Tradition says that she was busy sweeping on the night the Three Kings came searching for the Christ Child. They asked her to journey on with them, but she refused. Later, when the work was done, Befana shouldered her broom and set out for Bethlehem. Alone, she lost her way and so she searches for the Child forever.

The story traveled far to the north and to the east. In old Russia it was Babouschka who brought gifts. Like Befana she was a poor, little, crooked, wrinkled old woman. And like Befana she had refused to go with the Kings, and now searches for the Infant Jesus. Over the world she travels, peering in every cradle and leaving presents for little children as she sadly wanders on.

In Spain the legend of Berchta took yet another form, for Spain, too, was overrun by Germanic tribes in the fifth century. Berchta herself was gradually forgotten, but one of her companions lived on. The gift-bringer was a shadowy being, dark or black, as befitted one who long had traveled with a witchlike goddess.

But Spain was invaded many times, and its legends changed accordingly. In the eighth century the Moors came, Moslems from northern Africa. Most of the new conquerors were brown-skinned Arabs and Berbers, but among them were black men from south of the Sahara desert. For the Spaniards, black could now mean African, and the dark gift-bringer acquired a new identity.

Medieval legend had named the Three Kings who brought gifts to the Christ Child. They were Gaspar, Melchior and Balthasar, and artists invariably pictured Balthasar as an African, a king of Ethiopia. So now two legendary black men traveled about Spain at the end of each year: Berchta's companion, who brought gifts to the children, and Balthasar, who had brought gifts to the Christ Child. Inevitably the two were confused. As generation succeeded generation, it became Balthasar who rode through the land at night, Balthasar who left sweets for good children and marked their faces with charcoal, so that they could know that the black king had come. Finally the darkness of the gift-bringer became incidental, its importance long forgotten. Today it is all three kings, splendid and regal upon their camels, who bring gifts in Spain on the twelfth day after Christmas.

In the meantime, while Berchta was acquiring new names and new, unlikely companions, the tribes that had remained in Germany finally were giving up paganism and becoming fully Christian. By the tenth century the ancient gods and goddesses could no longer be tolerated, even as rivals of the Christian god. But old customs die hard. Berchta had always watched over the children, had always visited them in December. If Berchta was gone, they needed a new protector. In time St. Nicholas filled the role.

Who was this Nicholas? Legends are plentiful but facts are few. Most probably he lived at the end of the fourth century or the beginning of the fifth. Tradition says he was a much-loved bishop of Myra, in Asia Minor. At that time Myra was a bustling city, part of the Roman Empire. Today, its name changed to Demre, it is a sleepy little village in modern Turkey. The ancient church in Demre still stands, and in it lies a broken sarcophagus, said to have been the original tomb of St. Nicholas.

Popular devotion to Nicholas grew rapidly after his death. Legends increased the number of his followers, and his followers increased the number of his legends. His fame spread northward to the new Christians of Kiev, in Russia, and in time he became the patron of all of Russia. Sailors, too, claimed Nicholas as their patron, and devotion to the saint spread all around the shores of the Mediterranean Sea.

In 1087 Italian sailors moved the remains of Nicholas from Myra to Bari, in southern Italy. The remains were stolen, the people of Myra claimed. They were rescued from possible harm by the Turks, the Italians replied. At any rate, Nicholas had a new tomb in Bari, and a beautiful basilica was built over it. From Bari his fame spread over all of western Europe. His feast day, December 6, became an official church holiday during the twelfth and thirteenth centuries. The devotion of the common people never faltered, never wandered. He was, next to the Virgin, the most popular saint in Christendom. Hundreds of churches and thousands of children were named for him. There were forty-five churches dedicated to Nicholas in the city of Rome alone, four hundred in England, and forty in far-off Iceland. So popular was the name that it survives as a surname in numerous languages: Nichols, Nicholson, Collins, Colson, Klaassen, Claesz, Clausen, Klasesz, Nielsen, Nijssen, Colijn and others.

How did this great saint of the Middle Ages come to take on Berchta's role? Legends linking Nicholas with children undoubtedly had much to do with it. One story told of the three young students who were killed by a wicked innkeeper and then brought back to life by Nicholas. There was also a story of a baby who was miraculously unharmed by scalding bathwater, thanks to the intercession of the good saint. And there was a story of a child of Myra, Basilios by name, who was kidnapped by Arab pirates and enslaved. He despaired of ever being rescued, but one night he found himself being gathered up by Nicholas, as if in a dream, and then safely set down in his own courtyard. Whether the legends inspired the patronage, or the patronage the legends, is impossible to say; but by the thirteenth century St. Nicholas was firmly established as the patron of children all over Europe.

Another, more famous legend clearly identified Nicholas as a gift-giver who came in secret. The story concerns a widower, a nobleman who lived in the same town as Nicholas. The man, once well-to-do, was penniless. He had three teen-age daughters, and no money with which to feed and clothe them, much less provide them with the dowries needed for marriage. Desperate and distraught, he decided he would have to sell his daughters into slavery.

Nicholas, not yet a bishop or even a priest, had inherited a large fortune from his parents. He heard of the man's predicament. Determined to help but unwilling to identify himself, he tied three hundred gold florins in a square of cloth. After dark he went up to the nobleman's house and threw the coins in through an open window. The money provided the oldest daughter with a dowry and allowed the rest of the family to get along for some time. When the money was gone, Nicholas repeated his kind act and the second daughter married. Finally Nicholas came again, with money for a dowry for the third daughter. This time the father caught him and thanked him profusely. Nicholas, embarrassed, insisted that he tell no one; but years later, after his death, the story was revealed.

St. Nicholas's feast day came in December. Berchta's annual pilgrimage occurred in the same month. Gradually, as so often happened in newly Christian Europe, the identities became fused and Nicholas came to assume Berchta's functions.

A new ritual was established throughout much of western Europe. Each year, on the night of December 5, the eve of his feast day, Nicholas was believed to travel over the land. Dressed in elaborate ecclesiastical robes, he nevertheless rode across the sky on a white or pale gray horse, as Woden and Berchta had done before him. He came to the home of every child, bringing gifts and sweets for the good and obedient, and the rod, or birch switches, for the bad. There was no doubt he was a bishop and a saint, but still he was drawn to the hearth. It was there that the children's shoes or, later, stockings were placed; and it was there that hay or grain was left for his horse. At first he came in secret. In some communities he later came openly, with dignity, and questioned all the children about their behavior during the previous year. As befitted a bishop, he often asked if prayers had been learned and listened to catechism lessons.

But for all the emphasis on Christianity, the pagan past still intruded. Almost always Nicholas was accompanied by a small creature that was never clearly identified. Sometimes he was dark, sometimes covered with fur. Occasionally he had horns. Usually he was ugly. In some places the rods and switches were attributed to this creature rather than to Nicholas, and it was said that really wicked children might be carried off by him and not returned to their parents for a year. In other places the creature was given the task of sliding down the chimney, since it was not fitting for the bishop to soil his fine robes. The pagan goddess Berchta was gone, but a remnant of her band of elves and dwarfs lingered on.

Then, during the sixteenth-century period known as the Reformation, new Protestant churches were established in many of the countries of Europe. Devotion to the Roman Catholic saints was vigorously suppressed. The reformers preached that all good things came directly from God. Nicholas had to be dethroned as Berchta had been before him. If the children were to receive gifts, they should be taught that they came from the Christ Child.

The new idea had a charm and attractiveness of its own. Gradually St. Nicholas's Day was pushed aside and gifts began to come on Christmas Eve. In parts of France it was *Le Petit Jesus* (the little Jesus) who brought the treats; in southern Germany and much of Switzerland it was the *Christkindl*. The word means "Christ Child," and in some communities the Infant Jesus himself was said to come in secret, laden with gifts. In others the *Christkindl* came to be thought of as an angel child sent down from heaven. The angel often was portrayed as a young girl, tall and slim, with flowing robes and large golden wings. She wore a golden crown upon her long blond curls.

The idea of the *Christkindl* was brought to America by German immigrants, but its original religious identity was lost. The word was changed to Kris Kringle, and became simply another name for Santa Claus.

Elsewhere in Europe, other gift-bringers filled in for the out-of-favor St. Nicholas. Father Christmas or *Père Noël*, *Knecht Rupert*, *Pelznickel*, *Ru-Klas*, the *Schimmelreiter* and even Berchta herself joined the Christmas celebrations. Many of these personages had had a shadowy existence of their own for centuries before the Reformation. Father Christmas or *Père Noël* was a personification of the Christmas feast, perhaps originally a substitute for Woden or Saturn. The *Knecht Rupert* had been Nicholas's servant; before that he had been Berchta's bondsman. *Pelznickel* means "fur-Nicholas," a combination of the old saint and his little pagan companion. *Ru-Klas* is literally "rough Nicholas"; Nicholas could remain if he was no longer a saint or clad in bishop's robes. *Schimmelreiter* means "gray-horse rider," his actual identity as Woden or Berchta or Nicholas purposely covered over. Berchta, of course, needs no explanation. Deprived of their beloved St. Nicholas, the Germans simply resurrected the ancient goddess. In the provinces of Alsace and Lorraine, she wore the flaming headdress traditionally seen on St. Lucia. To the north, in the Scandinavian countries, *Jul* elves brought the gifts. Once, of course, they too had been part of Berchta's band.

Nicholas was not easily destroyed, however. His influence remained strong in Belgium, Austria, Czechoslovakia and, most especially, in the Netherlands.

In Czechoslovakia children believed that Nicholas climbed down from heaven on a golden rope to distribute gifts on Christmas Eve. He was accompanied by an angel with white wings, and by a black devil named Cert, who carried a whip and rattled a chain to frighten children who misbehaved.

In the Netherlands, once part of the Spanish empire, the good bishop came not from heaven, but from Spain. It was due to this Spanish influence, no doubt, that his companion became *Zwarte Piet* (Black Peter), a young African boy handsomely dressed as a medieval page.

By the eighteenth century the Nicholas tradition seemed complete in Europe. In America, however, it was just beginning.

Nineteenth-century historians believed that devotion to St. Nicholas came to New Amsterdam (now New York) with the first Dutch settlers in 1624, and that his feast day was enthusiastically celebrated there each and every December after that. Modern historians dispute the point, arguing that there is very little evidence to support the claim. Both church and state in the little American colony were thoroughly Protestant. No doubt any open celebration of a saint's feast day would have been severely frowned on. If St. Nicholas was alive and well and living in New Amsterdam throughout the colonial period, he must often have been driven underground.

It was in the period just after the American Revolution that Nicholas came into his own in New York. All things British were out of fashion and New Yorkers were paying much more attention to their Dutch heritage. John Pintard, who founded the New-York Historical Society in 1804, was a man who loved holidays. It is due largely to his efforts that the United States celebrates Washington's Birthday and the Fourth of July. He also must be credited with interesting New Yorkers of all nationalities in the early Dutch *Sinter Claes* (*Sint* meaning "saint," *Claes*, a shortened form of "Nicholas"). Patiently he gathered together the few remaining traditions about the saint. There was not much left to find, but he did succeed in getting the words to an old Dutch children's hymn that began "*Sancte Claus, goed heylig man*" (*Sancte* from the Latin *sanctus*, meaning "saint"; *goed heylig man*, Dutch for "good holy man"). The hymn ended with a plea for gifts and a promise of utmost loyalty. Pintard had the hymn translated and distributed widely, along with a picture of the saintly Nicholas. Pintard's *Sancte Claus* was still dressed as a bishop, and still brought switches as well as gifts, but he usually came on Christmas Eve, not December 5.

St. Nicholas's American following was further encouraged by the author Washington Irving. In 1809 Irving wrote "Diedrich Knickerbocker's" *History of New York from the Beginning of the World to the End of the Dutch Dynasty*. It was not really a history, but a crazy mixture of fact and fiction. New Yorkers found it delightful, and it was widely read. In the book Irving constantly makes mention of St. Nicholas as the patron of the little Dutch colony. Irving's Nicholas is no bishop from Asia Minor but a sturdy Dutchman, wearing a low, broad-brimmed hat and smoking a pipe. He claimed that a figurehead of Nicholas adorned the first ship to bring colonists from the Netherlands, and that the good saint appeared in a dream and urged them to settle at the tip of Manhattan Island. According to Irving, St. Nicholas's Day was always observed in the tiny colony, and each December 5 the saint rode over the tops of the trees in a wagon filled with gifts. Irving introduced St. Nicholas to many Americans who had never heard of him before, and prompted a new wave of interest in him.

One man who certainly read Irving's *History* was Clement Clarke Moore. Moore was a professor of Greek and Hebrew at the General Theological Seminary in New York City. A learned man, serious, perhaps even solemn, he was also the father of six small children, and he liked to write verse. Some time in December of 1822 he wrote a Christmas poem for his young sons and daughters, all of whom were under seven years of age. That Christmas Eve he read it aloud to his family.

It was brief and lively enough to hold the attention of even the youngest:

'Twas the night before Christmas, when all
        through the house
Not a creature was stirring, not even a mouse;
The stockings were hung by the chimney with care,
In hopes that St. Nicholas soon would be there;
The children were nestled all snug in their beds,
While visions of sugar-plums danced in their heads;
And Mamma in her 'kerchief, and I in my cap,
Had just settled our brains for a long winter's nap,
When out on the lawn there arose such a clatter,
I sprang from the bed to see what was the matter.
Away to the window I flew like a flash,
Tore open the shutters and threw up the sash.
The moon on the breast of the new fallen snow
Gave a lustre of mid-day to objects below,
When, what to my wondering eyes did appear,
But a miniature sleigh, and eight tiny reindeer.
With a little old driver, so lively and quick,
I knew in a moment it must be St. Nick.
More rapid than eagles his coursers they came,
And he whistled, and shouted, and called them by name;
"Now, Dasher! now, Dancer! now, Prancer and Vixen!
On, Comet! on, Cupid! on, Donner and Blitzen!
To the top of the porch! to the top of the wall!
Now dash away! dash away! dash away all!"
As dry leaves that before the wild hurricane fly,
When they meet with an obstacle, mount to the sky,
So up to the house-top the coursers they flew,
With the sleigh full of toys, and St. Nicholas too.
And then, in a twinkling, I heard on the roof
The prancing and pawing of each little hoof.
As I drew in my head, and was turning around,

Down the chimney St. Nicholas came with a bound,
He was dressed all in fur, from his head to his foot,
And his clothes were all tarnished with ashes and soot;
A bundle of toys he had flung on his back,
And he looked like a peddler just opening his pack.
His eyes—how they twinkled! His dimples, how merry!
His cheeks were like roses, his nose like a cherry!
His droll little mouth was drawn up like a bow,
And the beard on his chin was as white as the snow;
The stump of a pipe he held tight to his teeth,
And the smoke it encircled his head like a wreath;
He had a broad face and a little round belly,
That shook when he laughed, like a bowl full of jelly,
He was chubby and plump, a right jolly old elf,
And I laughed when I saw him, in spite of myself;
A wink of his eye and a twist of his head
Soon gave me to know I had nothing to dread.
He spoke not a word, but went straight to his work,
And filled all the stockings; then turned with a jerk,
And laying his finger aside of his nose,
And giving a nod, up the chimney he rose.
He sprang to his sleigh, to his team gave a whistle,
And away they all flew like the down of a thistle.
But I heard him exclaim ere he drove out of sight,
"HAPPY CHRISTMAS TO ALL, AND
TO ALL A GOODNIGHT."

The children were delighted, and the poet himself was quite satisfied with his Christmas effort. Yet no one in the room had the slightest idea that a vital piece of Christmas lore had been created.

Moore's St. Nicholas (for nowhere in the poem does he call him Santa Claus, although variations of the name were already in use) was pulled from many sources. Tidbits of the imagery —the pipe, the smoke, the "laying his finger aside of his nose"

—are taken directly from Irving's *History*. Quite likely it was Irving, too, who inspired Moore to make his Nicholas "chubby and plump," the very opposite of the lean, ascetic bishop shown in medieval paintings.

Moore was a scholar and well read. He must have known much more about European Christmas customs than did most Americans in the nineteenth century. Moore's "St. Nick" may have been a "right jolly old elf" because his creator was familiar with the *Jul* elves of Sweden and Denmark. And it was probably Germany's *Pelznickel* that caused him to be "dressed all in fur from his head to his foot."

Another early piece of Nicholas literature had appeared anonymously in New York in 1821, just one year before Moore wrote his verses. The poem was included in a children's book with simple illustrations. Here, for the first time, "Old Santeclaus" is shown riding not in a wagon but in a sleigh, pulled by a single reindeer. The identity of the illustrator is unknown. Whoever he was, he must have decided that a sleigh was more suitable than a wagon for one who traveled in the wintertime. Reindeer, too, were associated with snow and ice. Moore increased that one reindeer to eight and named them forever. The scholarly New Yorker had created an American St. Nicholas, as different from the European version as the New World was from the Old.

The image might easily have been lost, for Moore had no thought of publishing the verses. But some time after Christmas they were copied by a relative who then let a friend make a copy for herself. That friend was Harriet Butler, who lived in Troy, New York. She took the poem to the editor of the *Troy Sentinel*, who published it without the author's name in December 1823. If the editor knew who the poet was, he was not about to embarrass a distinguished New Yorker. He did give the verses a title: "An Account of a Visit from St. Nicholas," though the poem is referred to more often today as "The Night Before Christmas." The *New York Morning Courier* printed it in 1829; the *Schenectady Whig*, in 1832. The first illustrated version was prepared by Myron King, a Troy engraver, in the early 1830s, and countless others followed.

It was not until 1837 that Moore finally brought himself to acknowledge publicly that he was the author of "A Visit from St. Nicholas." It was included, with several of his other poems, in *The New-York Book of Poetry* published in that year. Moore rather apologetically included it in an anthology of his poems published in 1844. He probably never really understood the importance of his contribution to Christmas and to childhood. The rest of his poems are long forgotten.

The United States had its Santa Claus, but his physical appearance was still indistinct. It remained for yet another New Yorker to help Americans decide just what their beloved "St. Nick" really looked like. He was Thomas Nast, a German-born illustrator and cartoonist who was the creator of the Democratic party's donkey and the Republican's elephant.

Nast's first drawing of Santa Claus was done for a children's book published in 1863. It was followed by a series of Christmas drawings that appeared in *Harper's Weekly* magazine over the next twenty-three years. Nast's Santa was clearly based on Moore's. He was "chubby and plump," and "dressed all in fur from his head to his foot." His beard was "as white as the snow." He smoked a pipe, and he carried his "bundle of toys" in the proper manner, "flung on his back." But Nast also added details of his own, like the North Pole workshops where the toys were built, and a great book in which all children's names were recorded, along with notes on their behavior. His Santa kept an eye on the world through an old-fashioned hand-held telescope, and received letters from children, which he promptly answered.

Most of the artists and illustrators who followed Nast stayed within the tradition he had established, while the storytellers continued to add details. Mrs. Santa Claus made her first appearance in an 1889 book, *Goody Santa Claus on a Sleigh Ride*, by Katherine Lee Bates, who later wrote "America the Beautiful." And even before Nast's drawings, authors had begun to give Santa dozens of elves to help in his workshops. Perhaps they knew of Nicholas's European companions; more likely they just thought that someone as busy as Santa would need a great many helpers.

Santa's image was updated once more in the twentieth century. In 1931 Haddon Sundblom, a successful magazine illustrator, began a series of Santa paintings commissioned by the Coca-Cola Company for use in their December advertisements. Sundblom, like Nast, followed Moore's description closely, with one important exception. His Santa was robust, grandfatherly, and well over six feet tall. The elfin look had vanished entirely. With Sundblom's contributions, Santa Claus was complete.

Except—

Except for Rudolph the Red-Nosed Reindeer!

Rudolph was created in 1939, the brainchild of Robert May, a copywriter for Montgomery Ward and Company. The country was dragging itself out of the Great Depression and Ward's wanted something for their department-store Santas to hand out. May came up with a simple story about a reindeer with a red nose. Ward's gave away 2,400,000 copies of the booklet in 1939, and 3,600,000 when it was used again in 1946.

No longer interested in Rudolph, the company then gave the copyright of the story to May, who went looking for a publisher. Finally a small firm decided to chance a small printing. Two years later, in 1949, May sent the story to a songwriter, Johnny Marks. Marks wrote the song; Gene Autry, a cowboy-movie star, sang it; and Santa suddenly had a new companion, known all over the world.

For the American Santa had sailed back across the Atlantic Ocean. Clement Moore's poem eventually was published in most of the languages of western Europe, and Sundblom's Santa appeared in many different countries as the Coca-Cola Company sought to create an international market for their product.

In the havoc and destruction caused by World War II, Santa was all but forgotten. But after the war he reappeared in western Europe. Often he was introduced exuberantly by United States soldiers who provided Christmas parties for children in countless villages and towns. The kindness of the American GI made Santa known and loved everywhere, even in Japan with its very different culture. Except in the Netherlands, where loyalty to the traditional saintly bishop is strongest, the American Santa is rapidly replacing his ancestors, both Christian and pagan.

O CHRISTMAS TREE

O Christmas tree, O Christmas tree,
With faithful leaves unchanging;
Not only green in summer's heat,
But also winter's snow and sleet,
O Christmas tree, O Christmas tree,
With faithful leaves unchanging.

O Christmas tree, O Christmas tree,
Of all the trees most lovely;
Each year, you bring to me delight
Gleaming in the Christmas night.
O Christmas tree, O Christmas tree,
Of all the trees most lovely.

O Tannenbaum, O Tannenbaum,
Wie treu sind deine Blätter!
Du grünst nicht nur zur Sommerzeit,
Nein, auch im Winter, wenn es schneit.
O Tannenbaum, O Tannenbaum,
Wie treu sind deine Blätter!

O Tannenbaum, O Tannenbaum,
Du kannst mir sehr gefallen!
Wie oft hat mich zur Weihnachtszeit

Ein Baum von dir mich hoch erfreut!
O Tannenbaum, O Tannenbaum,
Du kannst mir sehr gefallen!

TRADITIONAL GERMAN CAROL,
translated by George K. Evans

Deck the Halls

NO OTHER holiday decoration is as well loved as the Christmas tree. Indeed, for countless families in Germany, the United States and a number of other countries, it is far more than a mere decoration. With its shining ornaments and glowing lights, it has become an essential part of the Christmas celebration.

The modern Christmas tree, gaily trimmed and lit, is not really very old—at least as compared to other Christmas customs—but it stems from four earlier practices that reach far back into European traditions.

The pagan Germans were a forest people with strong tendencies toward tree worship. Like the Romans, they valued evergreen trees as a sign of life in a barren, freezing world—a sign that spring and fruitfulness would return to the land. Branches were brought inside to provide shelter from the cold for the wood sprites who were believed to dwell in trees. In some places small trees, too, were cut down and brought inside.

Very little is known about these Yule trees. Apparently they had no more religious significance than the branches, and they were not decorated. Nevertheless, they existed, and almost certainly were the beginning of the association of fir trees with Christmas.

The flowering branch was another forerunner of the Christmas tree. Since Roman times European peoples had cut cherry branches and brought them inside, hoping to force them into bloom for the winter holidays. December 4, St. Barbara's Day, was considered the proper time to begin the project, which took considerable skill in poorly heated peasants' huts. Success was believed to bring good luck. The girl who could produce blooms exactly on Christmas Eve was sure to find a good husband within a year. Even if she did not, a branch covered with blossoms was a beautiful sight on Christmas morning.

Other customs reinforced the idea of a holiday tree. In many parts of Europe, plays were enacted during the Christmas season. Besides the mummers' crude skits, there were religious dramas. The church for centuries used "mystery plays" or "miracle plays" as a means of teaching the common people who could not read. Simple dramas based on scripture, they served to entertain as well as to educate. December 24, in the early church calendar, was the Feast of Adam and Eve, and in Germany the "Paradise play" was commonly performed on this day or earlier in the season of Advent. The play represented the creation of human beings, the sin of Adam and Eve and their expulsion from Paradise. It closed with a consoling promise of the coming savior, and was therefore a favorite pageant for the pre-Christmas season.

The staging for such plays was simple. Props were almost nonexistent, but the Paradise play did require an apple tree. In place of the winter-bare branches of a real fruit tree, a fir tree hung with apples was the obvious choice. Later, round white wafers were added to the tree to represent the bread used at the communion service in church and, by extension, Christ's redemption.

In at least some areas, the Paradise tree was imitated in the home, and pious Germans placed little figures of Adam and Eve and the serpent under their "Tree of Life."

Finally, and perhaps most important of all, there was the widespread custom of the Christmas pyramid. Beginning late in the Middle Ages, many homes in both Germany and Italy proudly displayed a holiday pyramid, a light wooden frame with several tiers of shelves, the whole decorated with candles, green branches and pretty baubles of every sort. In Germany this elaborate piece was called a *lichtstock* (light pole) and was quite clearly intended for use as a candelabrum. In Italy the pyramid was called a *ceppo* (log), probably a shortened form of *ceppo di Natale* (the Yule log); it has survived there in its original form, often with a crib scene on the first tier and tiny, gaily wrapped presents on the others.

Late in the sixteenth century these four traditions apparently came together, and the first decorated Christmas trees appeared in Germany, west of the Rhine River.

Laws restricting the cutting of trees at the Christmas season had been passed in the 1500s, but the first detailed description of a decorated tree is dated 1605. In a fragment of a travel diary an unidentified visitor to Strasbourg wrote, "At Christmas fir trees are set up in the rooms . . . and hung with roses cut from paper of many colors, apples, wafers, spangle-gold, sugar, etc."

Gradually the idea spread, but not always in the same form. In some parts of Germany the tree was hung upside down; in others it was right side up, but still suspended from the rafters. Finally the tree's trunk was firmly planted on solid ground, and it began to be more elaborately decorated.

Gilded nuts were an early addition, and the wafers of the Paradise tree turned into the Christmas cookies for which the Germans became famous. The earliest cookies were made in molds; later, cookie cutters were introduced, made by tinsmiths.

Hearts, bells, angels and stars were all popular shapes for Christmas cookies. These were usually made from white dough, while brown dough was preferred for the forms of people and animals.

Marzipan, the almond-paste confection originally from Persia, had been introduced in Europe after the Crusades. Long a luxury available only to the rich, a rising standard of living turned it into a Christmas treat for all. The German city of Lübeck made marzipan its specialty, and soon brilliantly colored fruits and vegetables made of the sweet paste began to appear on the tree. Eggshells were also among the earliest ornaments. Carefully broken in two and colored, the shells became delicate little baskets which were filled with tiny candies.

For a time the emphasis on edible ornaments was so great that the Christmas tree was called a "sugar tree." Children—far from dreading the dismantling of the tree on January 6—looked forward to it, for then the treats would be theirs to eat.

Pleasant as the new custom sounds, it was not at first accepted by everyone. Even in Strasbourg, which may well have been the original home of the Christmas tree, it met with bitter criticism. Dr. Johann Dannhauer, professor and preacher at the Strasbourg Cathedral, condemned the decorated tree roundly in a catechism published in the 1640s. He complained that

> among other trifles which are set up during Christmas time instead of God's word is the Christmas tree or fir tree which is put up at home and decorated with dolls and sweets . . . . Whence comes the custom, I know not: it is child's play . . . . Far better were it to point the children to the spiritual cedar-tree, Jesus Christ.

The condemnations went virtually unnoticed by the Christmas-loving Germans, and the tree continued to flourish. It was more quickly adopted by the rising middle class than by the poorer and more conservative peasants. In the areas of Germany where Lutheranism had become the established religion, the custom of decorating a tree spread quite rapidly and mistakenly has been attributed to Martin Luther himself. Acceptance came much more slowly in the southern, Catholic regions of Germany, where the people were reluctant to make anything but the crib scene the center of attention. Eventually, though, the tree became a vital part of Christmas throughout Germany; and in a land of forests no one was too poor to have one.

Early German Christmas trees were table-size. Only in America would the tree become a dazzling display stretching from floor to ceiling. In wealthy German homes trees were set up on small tables for each member of the family, and on each table were heaped that person's gifts and sweets.

The oldest known description of a tree decorated with candles comes from a sister-in-law of King Louis XIV of France. In a letter written in 1708, Liselotte von der Pfalz described the Christmas trees that she remembered from her German childhood:

> Tables are fixed up like altars, and outfitted for each child with all sorts of things, such as new clothes, silver, dolls, sugar candy, and so forth. Boxwood trees are set on the tables, and a candle is fastened to each branch.

Beautiful as the candles were, they presented a terrible fire hazard. In more cautious homes the tree was lit only once, on Christmas Eve, when the parlor doors were thrown open and the children saw the tree for the first time. Even then, some member of the family was stationed near the tree, holding a long pole with a wet sponge on the end, just in case one flickering flame might not have been placed as carefully as it should have been. Several buckets of water lined up against the wall provided some small measure of insurance in the event of a catastrophe.

The Christmas tree spread to other countries as Germans living abroad took their customs with them. Switzerland and Austria adopted it readily. By the middle of the nineteenth century, the decorated tree was a familiar sight at Christmas in the Scandinavian countries and in Russia, though in the latter country it was confined to the upper classes. Princess Helene of Mecklenburg, who came to France to marry the king's eldest son, introduced the tree in Paris in 1840. So quickly did the custom take hold that fifty years later, between thirty and thirty-five thousand trees were sold in Paris each year at the holiday season.

The Christmas tree came to England with the Hanoverians, the royal cousins from Germany who succeeded the childless Queen Anne in 1716. In 1761 the German Princess Charlotte married the almost-German King George III. Charlotte, who would become the mother of thirteen children, loved family holidays of any sort, and her Christmas was a typically German one. An eyewitness later remembered that

> in the middle of the room stood an immense tub with a yew tree placed in it, from the branches of which hung bunches of sweetmeats, almonds, raisins in papers, fruits, and toys, most tastefully arranged, and the whole illuminated by small wax candles.

Other German princesses coming to England to be queens kept up the tradition of the decorated tree. Adelaide, who married William IV in 1818, always had a tree for her Christmas Eve parties in the Dragon Room at Brighton Pavilion.

But these were royal trees, set up by German women who were perhaps a little homesick for their native land. They were hardly noticed by the English people, who were not overly fond of their hard-drinking Hanoverian kings.

A change took place in Queen Victoria's reign. She came to the throne in 1837, a young woman only eighteen years old, and captured the hearts of her subjects. Like so many of the Hanoverians, she too married a German—Albert of Saxe-Coburg-Gotha. But in her case both the royal wedding and the young couple's growing family enthralled the English people. Albert, remembering his happy childhood, wanted a German Christmas, and Victoria readily agreed. Trees provided by her German mother had been a part of her own youthful Christmases, and besides, to Victoria her husband's word was law. In 1841 Albert wrote to his father,

> This is the dear Christmas Eve, on which I have so often listened with impatience for your step, which was to usher us into the present room. Today I have two children of my own to give presents to, who, they know not why, are full of happy wonder at the German Christmas-tree and its radiant candles.

Seven years later the *Illustrated London News* featured a picture of the royal family gathered around their Christmas tree, and accompanied it with a glowing description:

> The Christmas tree is annually prepared by her Majesty's command for the Royal children. . . . The tree employed for this festive purpose is a young fir of about eight feet high, and has six tiers of branches. On each tier, or branch, are arranged a dozen wax tapers. Pendant from the branches are elegant trays, baskets, *bonbonnières*, and other receptacles for sweetmeats of the most varied and expensive kind; and of all forms, colours, and degrees of beauty. Fancy cakes, gilt gingerbread and eggs filled with sweetmeats, are also suspended by variously-colored ribbons from the branches. The tree, which stands upon a table covered with white damask, is supported at the root by piles of sweets of a larger kind, and by toys and dolls of all

> descriptions, suited to the youthful fancy . . . . On the summit of the tree stands the small figure of an angel, with outstretched wings, holding in each hand a wreath.

At once almost every middle-class family in England decided that they must have a tree, too. Albert encouraged the idea by presenting decorated trees to schools, army barracks and other institutions. It may have been a deliberate attempt to foster the custom; more likely he simply wanted to give others the opportunity to share his enjoyment of the tree. At any rate, Christmas trees suddenly appeared everywhere.

The author Charles Dickens, whose name will be forever linked with Christmas, made no mention of the tree in his famous story, *A Christmas Carol*, published in 1843; but he gave his readers a vivid description of the new English trees in a magazine article written in 1850.

> I have been looking, this evening, at a merry company of children assembled round that pretty German toy, a Christmas tree. The tree was planted in the middle of a great round table, and towered high above their heads. It was brilliantly lighted by a multitude of little tapers; and everywhere sparkled and glittered with bright objects. There were rosy-cheeked dolls, hiding behind green leaves; and there were real watches (with movable hands, at least, and an endless capacity of being wound up) dangling from innumerable twigs; there were French polished tables, chairs, bedsteads, wardrobes, eight-day clocks, and various other articles of domestic furniture (wonderfully made in tin) perched among the boughs, as if in preparation for some fairy housekeeping; there were jolly, broad-faced little men, much more agreeable in appearance than many real men—and no wonder, for their heads took off, and showed them to be full of sugarplums; there were fiddles and drums; there were tambourines, books, work boxes,

> paint boxes; there were trinkets for the elder girls, far brighter than any grown-up gold and jewels; there were baskets and pin cushions in all devices; there were guns, swords and banners; there were witches standing in enchanted rings of pasteboard, to tell fortunes; there were teetotums [a child's toy similar to a top but spun by the fingers instead of string], humming tops, needle cases, pen wipers, smelling bottles, conversation cards, bouquet holders, real fruit, made artificially dazzling with gold leaf; imitation apples, pears, walnuts, crammed with surprises: in short, as a pretty child before me delightedly whispered to another pretty child, her bosom friend, "There was everything, and more." This motley collection of odd objects clustering on the tree like magic fruit, and flashing back the bright looks directed towards it from every side—some of the diamond eyes admiring it were hardly on a level with the table, and a few were languishing in timid wonder on the bosoms of pretty mothers, aunts, and nurses—made lively realisation of the fancies of childhood; and set me thinking how all the trees that grow and all the things that come into existence on the earth, have their wild adornments at that well remembered time.

Legend says that the Hessians, the German soldiers hired by the British to fight in the American Revolution, had the first Christmas trees in America; but historians have never been able to substantiate the claim. The first definite descriptions of decorated trees came from Pennsylvania, where many German colonists had settled. Scattered references to Christmas trees in rural areas there appeared in the early 1820s. In 1825 Philadelphia's *Saturday Evening Post* described

> trees visible through the windows, whose green boughs are laden with fruit, richer than the golden apples of the Hesperides, or the sparkling diamonds that clustered on the branches in the wonderful cave of Aladdin.

Later, German immigrants introduced the trees in other parts of the country. In Boston, Charles Follen, a German who taught at Harvard University, set up a tree for his son in 1832. Follen, who had been driven away from Germany in the upheavals of the 1820s, had made many friends in America. One of them, the popular English writer Harriet Martineau, described the tree in detail:

> My little friend Charley [Follen's son] and three companions had been long preparing for this pretty show. The cook had broken eggs carefully in the middle for some weeks past, that Charley might have the shells for cups; and these cups were gilded and coloured very prettily. We were all engaged in sticking on the last seven dozen of wax tapers, and in filling the gilded egg-cups and gay paper cornucopiae with comfits, lozenges, barley sugar. The tree was the top of a young fir, planted in a tub, which was ornamented with moss. Smart dolls and other whimsies glittered in the evergreen, and there was not a twig which had not something sparkling upon it.
>
> It really looked beautiful; the room seemed in a blaze, and the ornaments so well hung on that no accident happened, except that one doll's petticoat caught fire. There was a sponge tied to the end of a stick to put out any supernumerary blaze, and no harm ensued. I mounted the steps behind the tree to see the effect of opening the doors. It was delightful. The children poured in, but in a moment every voice was hushed. Their faces were upturned to the blaze, all eyes wide open, all lips parted, all steps arrested. Nobody spoke, only Charley leaped for joy. The first symptom of recovery was the children's wandering around the tree. At last, a quick pair of eyes discovered that it bore something eatable, and from that moment the babble began again . . . . I have little doubt the Christmas tree will become one of the most flourishing exotics of New England.

A year later Gustave Koerner, a German settler living in St. Clair County, Illinois, made do with a much simpler tree. Since there were no evergreens in the area, he and his friends decorated the bare branches of a sassafras tree with candles, apples, sweets, ribbons, bright paper, hazlenuts and even red haws, the sour little fruit of the hawthorn tree.

The first Christmas tree in Williamsburg, Virginia, appeared in 1842. Charles Minnigerode, a young, German-born teacher at the College of William and Mary, decorated a small evergreen tree to amuse the children of his friend, Professor Nathaniel Beverly Tucker. Minnigerode, lacking proper holders, wired the candles in place and decorated the tree with strings of popcorn, gilded nuts, bits of colored paper and a gold star.

As German settlers pushed west, they took the custom of the tree with them. One visitor to Texas in 1846 reported seeing "a richly decorated and illuminated Christmas tree . . . where . . . scarcely two years ago the camp fires of the wild Comanches were burning."

But these were all German trees, set up by German families. Only gradually did the custom spread among other Americans as well. In 1850 *Godey's Lady's Book*, the foremost women's magazine in America, ran the picture of Queen Victoria and her family's tree that had appeared in the *Illustrated London News* two years earlier. Americans, with no royalty of their own, quite worshiped the pretty young queen, and to have a tree like Victoria's suddenly became the new fashion.

Harriet Martineau's description of Follen's tree, appearing in a pamphlet published by the American Sunday School Union at Boston, also did much to spread the idea. Many children enjoyed a tree at school or church long before they had one at home.

For a time not everyone was enthusiastic about trees in the

home, anyway. One problem involved the gifts. The German custom was to place gifts among the branches; in the United States it was customary to fill stockings hung by the fireplace. To solve the problem most families began to put gifts in both places.

President Franklin Pierce had a Christmas tree in 1856, the first in the White House. Americans, always in a hurry, even form traditions quickly. Just thirty-five years later another president, Benjamin Harrison, could assure newspaper reporters that he would "have an old-fashioned Christmas tree for the grandchildren upstairs."

The early trees in the United States, like their European counterparts, were mostly trimmed with good things to eat. To the traditional nuts, apples and cookies of Germany were added strings of popcorn and strings of cranberries. The comfits and sweetmeats so often mentioned in early descriptions were usually candied fruits. Sugarplums, made famous in Moore's poem, could be greengage plums boiled in sugar syrup until they were crystallized. More often, however, the term was used for soft candies made of fondant, rather like the French bonbon. Hard candies, too, were popular. The candy cane, which in Europe had represented a shepherd's crook, was easy to place on the tree, and soon candymakers offered lengths of tiny candies already strung.

Commercially made ornaments—not toys, but pretty things meant to be saved from year to year—began to appear in the United States in the 1870s. Among the earliest were the silver and gold embossed cardboard ornaments made in and around the beautiful old German city of Dresden. Animals and fish were favorite subjects. Since the ornaments were three-dimensional, they were surprisingly attractive and realistic. Tinsel icicles, made of thin strips of silver foil, were originated in Nuremberg, in southern Germany, in 1878; they were an immediate success in the United States. *Engelshaar*, clouds of glistening strands that were supposed to look like angel's hair, started to come from Germany in the 1880s.

Color printing, which began in the 1830s, had become a highly developed art by the 1860s. German printers specialized in beautiful colored, highly sentimental little figures, which were embossed and stamped out by the same machine. Collecting these "scraps" and mounting them in "scrapbooks" became a fad both in Europe and the United States, but the scraps printed for the Christmas trade often were used as tree ornaments. Blond angels with long, flowing hair, and the old-fashioned German St. Nicholas or *Weihnachtsmann* (Christmas man) were especially popular. Sometimes they were pasted onto cookies with sugar frosting, or used to decorate homemade candy cornucopias, but often the figures were simply placed on the tree and enjoyed for their own sake

Attractive as all these decorations were, however, none ever rivaled the popularity of the shining, fragile, blown-glass ornaments that still are favorites.

Lauscha, a tiny village high in the Thuringian mountains in Germany, produced almost all the blown-glass ornaments sold in the United States until World War II. The glassmaking industry was brought to Lauscha in the 1590s, when religious persecution in the German province of Swabia forced little groups of Protestant glassmakers to leave their homes. They were drawn to the Thuringian mountains by an abundance of wood, sand and limestone, the necessary ingredients for their craft. By the early 1800s the glassblowers of Lauscha, working for the most part in their own homes, were supplying glass beads for jewelers and milliners all over Europe. Then, in 1857, rival glassblowers in Bohemia developed a silver-nitrate solution that gave their beads a brilliant, mirrorlike, silver luster.

Almost overnight Lauscha lost most of its bead market to

the Bohemian competition, and the town went into an economic depression. Fortunately a Lauscha glassmaker, Louis Greiner-Schlotfeger, succeeded in duplicating the Bohemians' silver formula. Almost single-handedly, he saved what was left of the town's bead business and laid the groundwork for manufacturing the Christmas tree ornaments that would replace beads and almost every other product made in the town.

In 1867 a gasworks was built in Lauscha. Now the glassblowers could work with a steady, easily adjustable gas flame. This made it possible for them to produce large, thin-walled bubbles of glass. Someone, very possibly the same Louis Greiner-Schlotfeger, discovered that the bubbles of glass could be blown into a mold. Soon silvered glass pinecones, apples, pears and crystal icicles were being sold in Germany and exported to the United States and other countries. Suddenly all of Lauscha was in the ornament business. It was a cottage industry. Whole families worked in their own homes, often for ten to fifteen hours a day, and for what amounted to very little money. The glassblower blew the ornaments while others in the family, including his wife and children, silvered them on the inside, lacquered them on the outside, cut them off cleanly from their stems, and added little metal caps.

Hard as the work was, the glassblowers took great pride in their craft. Most difficult to blow were the ornate glass treetops. Up to fourteen inches long, they were a graduated series of balls, one above another, with a spike on top. The whole thing was blown from one piece of glass tubing.

If the treetops were the most spectacular ornaments, those blown into molds were the most fascinating. Hoping to please the wholesalers who purchased their wares, the glassblowers of Lauscha experimented constantly with new designs. The apples and pears of the earliest years were joined by fruits and vegetables of every sort, including carrots, ears of corn and even pickles. Dogs, clowns, angels, fish and birds—the last always with tails of spun glass—were produced year after year. Pine cones and acorns were favorites, as were drums and violins, hearts and tiny houses and churches. Angels were popular and so were Santas, both the chubby American version and the thinner German type. Occasionally even the little humpbacked figure of Berchta was included, greatly puzzling American children who could not understand what a witch was doing on a Christmas tree.

Other blowers, working without molds, formed tiny teapots and attached miniature spouts and handles to them. Trumpets, too, were free-blown. A tiny whistle in the trumpet's stem allowed it to produce a single note, and there were bells that rang with a delicate tinkling sound.

World War I interrupted the trade, and after the war the German craftsmen faced severe competition from Japan and Czechoslovakia. The glassblowers persevered through the worldwide depression of the 1930s, but were then confronted with another war. The ornament industry in Lauscha never recovered from World War II. Borders drawn after the war placed the city ten miles inside East Germany, where the Soviet-dominated government discouraged trade with the United States or Western Europe. Attempts to reestablish the craft in West Germany failed. Young people had little interest in hot, tedious work at low pay. A small factory has been established in Lauscha and some of the old molds are still used, but very few of the ornaments are exported.

Production of glass ornaments in the United States began in the 1930s when Hitler's rise to power in Germany made it obvious that the world would be plunged into war a second time. Machines at the Corning Glass Company's plant in Wellsboro, Pennsylvania, could make more ornaments in a minute than a Lauscha glassblower could make in a day. Today, most of the familiar shining globes are made there. A few different shapes are also produced, but no attempt has been made to duplicate the glistening fairyland that once was created in Lauscha.

The charm of the hand-blown German ornaments was matched by the beauty of the flickering candles of the same period, but at a terrible price. Old newspaper accounts tell of tragic fires almost every year, especially as the candle-lit tree came to be featured at crowded Sunday-school and hospital children's ward parties. Perhaps the lighted trees would have been given up entirely if Thomas Edison had not invented the electric light in 1879. Three years later Edward H. Johnson, the vice-president of Edison's electric light company, had in his own home the first Christmas tree lit by electricity. It was an elaborate affair that featured blinking bulbs in three colors, and a stand, also powered by electricity, that turned the tree slowly round and round. The idea caught on at once among wealthy families who could afford to have a tree hand-wired for the occasion. In 1895 President Grover Cleveland added electric lights to the White House tree, much to the delight of his children, or so the newspapers said.

The Ever-Ready Company of New York pioneered in manufacturing and marketing strings of ready-made lights, and soon other companies entered the field. These early lights were of the "series" type. If one bulb burned out, all the others went off and someone painstakingly had to search the length of the set, dodging ornaments while testing for the "bad" bulb. "Parallel" wiring, which avoided this problem, was developed by the General Electric Company in 1927, but it did not come into general use until after World War II.

Each year the tree has become a more important part of the Christmas scene in the United States. The first outdoor Christmas tree with electric lights was set up in Pasadena, California, in 1909. Another followed in New York in 1912, and another in Philadelphia the following year. In 1923 President Calvin Coolidge lit the first outdoor tree at the White House. It was a gift from Coolidge's home state of Vermont. From 1923 to 1973 a tree was brought to Washington each year from a different state. In 1973 a tree was planted in an area south of the White House known as the Ellipse. It was hoped that it would grow and serve for years to come. Unfortunately, that tree died during 1977, and a new tree had to be planted for Christmas of that year.

In 1954 President Dwight D. Eisenhower expanded the ceremony of lighting the nation's Christmas tree and invited delegates from twenty-seven foreign embassies to participate in a "Pageant of Peace." This international exchange is now an important part of the annual holiday observance.

The use of outdoor trees, begun in the United States, has spread to other countries. The people of Norway, wishing to express appreciation for the aid given them in World War II, sent a giant tree to England in 1947. Beautifully lit, it was placed in London's Trafalgar Square, and the Norwegians have continued to send a tree each year.

Popular as the tree has proven, however, it is not the only Christmas plant. Other plants that retain their leaves in winter have come to be associated with the holiday season.

Without a doubt mistletoe has the longest history of any of the growing things associated with Christmas. Once held sacred by all European peoples, the small plant grows as a parasite, clinging to the highest branches of oaks and other trees. Curiously, the Ainu, the early Caucasoid people of northern Japan, also believed the mistletoe to be a magical plant. This could suggest that belief in the power of the mistletoe is incredibly ancient; the Ainu have lived in Japan for more than seven thousand years, and must have separated from the people who would become the Europeans at a far earlier time. On the other hand, it could be simply that many peoples have felt a superstitious awe for a plant that never touches the ground.

Mistletoe was most prominent in the religion of the Celts, the early inhabitants of the British isles. Pliny the Elder, the Roman naturalist who wrote in the first century, describes in detail how mistletoe was cut by the Druids, the Celtic priests. The ceremony, which came at the time of their New Year, apparently took place in a grove of oaks.

> Having made all due preparation for the sacrifice and a banquet beneath the trees, they bring thither two white bulls, the horns of which are bound for the first time. Clad in a white robe the priest ascends the tree, and cuts the mistletoe with a golden sickle, which is received by others in a white cloak.

The animals were then sacrificed, and apparently the mistletoe was distributed to the people.

Over the course of the centuries feelings about mistletoe, as about so many other things, went from sacred to magical to playful. Just how the custom of kissing under the mistletoe originated is uncertain. That it was a pale northern reflection of the hilarity of the *Saturnalia* has been suggested, but it seems unlikely since the practice is almost unknown except in England and in countries originally settled by English colonists. In the Celtic languages mistletoe was, and is, called "all-heal." Certainly a physical remedy was meant—for the plant was commonly considered to be an antidote to all poisons—but the custom of kissing suggests an early rite of forgiveness. Mistletoe may first have been hung over the door as a symbol of welcome and friendship; in time the kiss of peace may have turned into a kiss in fun. But other, different, explanations are also possible.

A similar tradition persisted for centuries in a few hidden

valleys deep in the Austrian Alps. On New Year's Eve people would linger late in the inns, the walls and windows of which were decorated with green pine twigs. In the center of the main room hung a wreath of pine; in a dark corner hid a masked figure known as the "Sylvester," old and ugly, with a yellow beard and wreath of mistletoe. If a maiden happened to pass under the pine wreaths, the Sylvester would spring out and give her a rough kiss. When midnight came he was boisterously banished from the inn as a representative of the old year.

The named Sylvester is easily enough explained, for the word *silva* means "forest" in Latin. Furthermore, in the Christian calendar December 31 is the feast day of St. Sylvester, though clearly the character portrayed was more pagan than saintlike. The mention of mistletoe coupled with the idea of prankish kissing on New Year's Eve suggests that the two ideas might be related, modern survivals of some belief whose origin and meaning are apparently lost forever.

In England in the late eighteenth and early nineteenth centuries, mistletoe was given the care and decoration later lavished on the Christmas tree. A "kissing bunch" or "kissing ball" was constructed of two hoops, one thrust through the other. Each was garlanded with sprigs of green, decorated with colored ribbons, paper roses, apples and, later, oranges. Inside were placed three tiny figures to represent the crib scene. Finally mistletoe was carefully tied to the bottom of the ball, which was then hung in a prominent place.

In some areas the fun associated with the mistletoe was strictly limited. At each kiss a berry had to be removed from the hanging branch, and when the berries were gone the game was finished. Always more clearly identified with the pagan past than other Christmas greens, mistletoe is rarely seen in churches.

Other plants, too, have played an important part in Christmas festivities. Holly, ivy and rosemary were all favored in England during the Middle Ages. Originally, no doubt, they were chosen simply because they kept their green leaves all winter in the comparatively mild climate of the British Isles.

Holly would have been especially valued as a sign of fruitfulness for, like the mistletoe, it kept its berries as well as its leaves throughout the winter. Christian legends turned the prickly leaves and red berries, which resemble drops of blood, into a reminder of the crown of thorns worn by Christ; but enough superstitions surround holly to suggest that it was sacred in pagan days. Witches were believed to hate the plant and to flee from it, and it was also said to inspire prophetic dreams.

In at least one old English Christmas carol, holly and ivy are portrayed as antagonists, apparently representing the battle of the sexes. Holly is the man's plant, ivy the woman's, and the two argue merrily. In some counties of England a variation of the old idea persists. The prickly and nonprickly kinds of holly are distinguished as "he" and "she" holly, and tradition maintains that the type of holly brought into a house at Christmastime determines whether the wife or the husband will rule the household.

Rosemary, an herb belonging to the mint family, also was a favorite. Its attractive gray-green leaves and fresh, sweet, pinewoods scent made it a natural addition to the Christmas decorations.

In eastern Europe and in Scandinavia the emphasis at midwinter was not on evergreen plants, but on straw and wheat—as symbols of the coming spring, a new crop and a good harvest.

In Norway, Sweden and Denmark, farm families put out the best sheaves of wheat saved from harvesttime, often mounting them on tall poles. Today the wheat is meant to feed the birds;

once it was intended to placate the evil spirits that rushed through the land in the long dark nights of early winter. In Poland, Finland, Lithuania and the Ukraine, straw was placed on the floor or, more often, on the table over the heavy linen cloth. In Christian times it was said to be a reminder of the stable of Bethlehem; but earlier it was a charm, used to insure a good harvest in the coming year.

The poinsettia, native to Mexico, had been cultivated for centuries by the Aztec Indians who used it to make a reddish-purple dye. Franciscan priests living near Taxco, Mexico, in the seventeenth century seem to have been the first to include poinsettias in Christmas celebrations. They used them in their Nativity procession, the *Fiesta de Santa Pesebre*. The custom was described by Don Hernando Ruiz de Alarcón, of Taxco, in a letter to his brother, Spanish playwright Don Juan Ruiz de Alarcón.

The poinsettia took its name from Joel R. Poinsett of Charleston, South Carolina, who introduced the plant to this country in 1828 while he was serving as United States minister to Mexico. Poinsett, a former congressman, was an avid amateur botanist, and he gave plants to a number of friends interested in horticulture.

Nature made the poinsettia a Christmas flower for, like a number of other plants, it will only begin to set buds and produce flowers as winter nights become longer. In order to bloom at Christmas, the poinsettia must have fourteen continuous hours of darkness every day from October 1 until about December 15.

The potential of a winter-blooming plant with beautiful red bracts (the actual blossom is the small, inconspicuous center) was soon obvious to the owners of commercial nurseries. The Paul Ecke family of Encinitas, California, professional growers for three generations, introduced many new varieties. In 1975 approximately 25,000,000 poinsettia plants were produced in the United States, and the plant has become almost as popular in other parts of the world.

GO TELL IT
ON THE MOUNTAIN

When I was a seeker,
  I sought both night and day;
I asked the Lord to help me,
  And He showed me the way.

Go tell it on the mountain,
Over the hills and everywhere;
Go tell it on the mountain,
That Jesus Christ is born.

He made me a watchman,
  Upon the city wall;
And if I am a Christian,
  I am the least of all.

Go tell it on the mountain,
Over the hills and everywhere;
Go tell it on the mountain,
That Jesus Christ is born.

TRADITIONAL
AMERICAN SPIRITUAL

Christmas in a Changing World

EUROPE went through a great spiritual upheaval in the sixteenth century. The Protestant Reformation, begun by Martin Luther in Germany in the early 1500s, caused many changes in the daily life of the people. Luther himself was no enemy of Christmas, and in Germany the holiday went on with little disruption. Elsewhere on the Continent, however, new Protestant groups were anxious to rid themselves of anything associated with Catholicism, and criticized the day as worldly, pagan and idolatrous.

In England it was the Anglican faith that finally prevailed. Moderate in doctrines and practices, the Anglicans celebrated Christmas both reverently and merrily. But even this moderation was bitterly criticized by a minority of English men and women. Anxious to "purify" the English church, these people came to be known as Puritans.

Soon the quarrel between the Anglicans and the Puritans become political as well as religious. In arguments between the king and Parliament, the Anglicans supported the king and became known as Royalists, while the Puritans favored Parliament. The differences between these two groups erupted in civil war in 1642. The Puritans, led by Oliver Cromwell, won and the king, Charles I, was executed.

For ten years Parliament and Oliver Cromwell ruled England. Christmas suffered mightily, for the Puritans hated the holiday and opposed it with a vengeance that has never been surpassed. Their point of view was neatly summed up by Hezekiah Woodward, who said in a tract written in 1656, called "Christmas Day":

> The old Heathen's Feasting Day, in honor of Saturn their Idol-God, the Papist's Massing Day, the Profane Man's Ranting Day, the Superstitious Man's Idol Day, the Multitude's Idle Day, Satan's—that Adversary's—Working Day, the True Christian Man's Fasting Day . . . . We are persuaded, no one thing more hindereth the Gospel work all the year long, than doth the observation of that Idol Day once in a year, having so many days of cursed observation with it.

Determined to uproot anything that remained of the old religion, the Puritan Parliament in 1647 officially abolished Christmas in England, as well as a number of other holidays. Nothing should be celebrated but the Sabbath, and that in a godly way. Knowing, or perhaps only suspecting, the pagan origin of mincemeat, the Christmas pie rated a special condemnation. As an Anglican poet, John Taylor, noted somewhat cynically, the mere eating of one was enough to have a person arrested for committing "high Parliament treason."

The laws were not obeyed. Riots broke out so regularly in a number of towns that to some people they seemed almost a part of the Christmas celebration. The persecution was real; even Anglican church services were broken up by armed soldiers. But the day continued to be kept, at least quietly, behind locked doors.

The Royalists came back to power in England in 1660, and

a new king, Charles II, came to the throne. Now it was the Puritans who were harassed for their beliefs, while the rest of England enjoyed the lavish holiday of the Restoration period.

In Scotland the suppression of Christmas was more thorough. The merriment was shifted to New Year's Day, and Christmas was ignored until the twentieth century.

New Year's Eve in Scotland was called Hogmanay. The origin of the word is uncertain. It may stem from the Norman *hoguinané* or the French *aguillanneuf*—both of which are also names for December 31—but it probably is more closely related to "Hogunnas," the name used on the Isle of Man for November 1, the old Celtic New Year.

On New Year's Eve it was customary for poor children to swaddle themselves in sheets, doubled up in front so as to form a pocket, and then go along the streets in little bands, calling out "Hogmanay" at the door of wealthy homes. They expected, and generally received, a quarter of an oatcake, sometimes with cheese. The gift, too, was called "Hogmanay." It all sounds very like the "trick or treat" of Halloween and, indeed, the two may be related. The custom lasted till well into the nineteenth century and one of the little rhymes survives.

> Get up, goodwife, and shake your feathers,
> And dinna think that we are beggars;
> For we are bairns come out to play,
> Get up and gie's our hogmanay!

Children and adults alike stayed up to see the New Year in. Toasts were drunk, and good wishes exchanged. The next day was spent calling on friends and neighbors. At every home visitors were served little cakes and pastries in whatever abundance the family could afford.

In the dignified city of Edinburgh, a custom began that spread to both London and the United States. The traditional

New Year's Eve in Edinburgh was vividly described in 1893 by an elderly resident who remembered the holidays of his youth:

> Towards evening the thoroughfares become thronged with the youth of the city . . . . As the midnight hour approaches, drinking of healths becomes more frequent, and some are already intoxicated . . . . The eyes of the immense crowd are ever turned towards the lighted clock-face of "Auld and Faithfu'" Tron [Church], the hour approaches, the hands seem to stand still, but in one second more the hurrahing, the cheering, the hand-shaking, the health-drinking, is all kept up for as long as the clock continues to ring out the much-longed-for midnight hour. . . . The crowds slowly disperse, and . . . the first-footers are off and away.

The "first-footers" mentioned were the last remnant of a curious and probably ancient custom. Great importance was attached to the first visitor of the New Year. This "first-foot" or "lucky bird" must be a man or boy; a woman was said to bring bad luck. Often it was required that he be dark-haired, for a fair or red-haired person would bring disaster. This notion suggests the very early period when a dark people, akin to the Welsh, inhabited all the British isles and resented the fair, invading Celts. And often the "first-foot" brought small, symbolic gifts: coal for warmth, food for plenty, a coin for wealth. It was the old Roman idea all over again—a good beginning would make a good year.

In the meantime, Christmas had come to North America, brought by the first European settlers. The newly Christian Vikings may have celebrated the holiday, but much more is known of Christopher Columbus's misadventures. On Christmas Eve, 1492, his ship, the *Santa Maria,* struck a coral reef off the island of Hispaniola, in the Caribbean Sea. The next day was spent unloading the ruined ship. Columbus persuaded himself that the accident was providential—that he was meant to found a colony at this place—and he named the little settlement *La Navidad* in honor of the holy day.

A little more than a century later, in 1607, the English settlers at Jamestown spent their first Christmas starving, praying for food and a ship from England. By the next year things were better. Snowbound in a friendly Indian village, the ever-optimistic John Smith could write:

> Wherever an Englishman may be, and in whatever part of the world, he must keep Christmas with feasting and merriment! And, indeed, we were never more merry, nor fed on more plenty of good oysters, fish, flesh, wild fowl and good bread; nor never had better fires in England than in the dry, smoky houses of . . . Kecoughton.

The Pilgrims who settled in New England had a very different attitude. Like the Puritans at home in England, they saw no reason to celebrate Christmas. Their ship, the *Mayflower*, arrived at Plymouth Bay in December, 1620, perhaps the worst month in which to begin a settlement. Work began at once. Governor William Bradford wrote in his diary:

> Monday, the 25th day. Some to fell timber, some to saw, some to rive [split wood], and some to carry, so no man rested all that day. We went to work on Plymouth's first building, the Common House, construction of which began on Christmas Day.

A starving time followed, and half the little colony died. Finally spring came, and crops, and the first Thanksgiving. By the following December conditions were much improved. Another ship had brought reinforcements; many of these people were Anglicans, come to Plymouth not to worship as they pleased, but to better their fortunes in the new land.

Christmas Day brought conflict, as Governor Bradford again noted:

> On the day called Christmas-day, the Governor called them out to work, (as was usual), but most of this new company excused themselves, and said it went against their consciences to work on the day. So the Governor told them that if they made it a matter of conscience, he would spare them until they were better informed. So he led away the rest, and left them; but when they came home at noon from their work, he found them in the street at play, openly; some pitching the bar, and some at stool ball, and such like sports. So he went to them and took away their implements, and told them it was against his conscience that they should play and others work. If they made the keeping of it a matter of devotion, let them keep to their houses, but there should be no gameing or revelling in the streets. Since which time nothing has been attempted that way, at least, openly.

Bradford was not really angry. He saw the funny side, for he called it an event "rather of mirth than of weight," but the Pilgrims' distaste for Christmas persisted, and hardened into law.

In 1659 the General Court of Massachusetts forbade, at the penalty of five shillings per offense, the observation of "any such day as Christmas or the like, either by forbearing of labour, feasting, or any such way." Connecticut, in the same period, prohibited the reading of Common Prayer, the keeping of Christmas or saints' days, the making of mince pies, playing at cards or performing on any instruments of music. Such laws were gradually repealed, but the New Englander's dislike of Christmas continued until well into the 1800s. The attitude is more easily understood if one remembers that throughout the colonial period royal governors from England constantly tried to thrust an established Anglican church upon a people who did not want it. For the men and women of early New England, any hint of keeping Christmas would have meant going over to the side of the enemy, and betraying their own faith.

But Christmas in America flourished in the South. The little colony at Jamestown grew into Virginia, the "Old Dominion," with a prosperous, even lavish, way of life, and Christmases to match.

The day itself was kept rather simply. Church services in the morning were followed by a fine dinner for the family in the late afternoon. In between times the men and boys welcomed Christmas with countless shots fired into the air and firecrackers by the hundreds.

But for well-to-do Virginians, Christmas lasted for a full twelve days. There was time aplenty for an almost endless round of partying. Plantation families would spend at least a few days with friends and relatives on neighboring estates. Fox hunts and balls entertained the visitors. Dancing was a passion with wealthy Virginians. Almost every fine home had a ballroom, or a large banquet room that could quickly be cleared for a dance. The minuet was the rage in London, and it soon came to the colonies. The lively and popular English dance, "Sir Roger de Coverley," would eventually turn into an American dance, the Virginia Reel. The Christmas season was also favored for courting, and for weddings. George Washington and Martha Custis were married on Twelfth Day in 1759, and Thomas Jefferson took Martha Skelton as his bride on New Year's Day, 1772.

Crowds of festive visitors had to be fed, and the quantities of food prepared in the plantation kitchens were prodigious. Martha Washington's Great Cake, really a fruit cake, is a stunning example. Handed down by her grandchildren and preserved at Washington's home, Mount Vernon, in Virginia, the recipe reads:

> Take 40 eggs and divide the whites from the yolks and beat them to a froth. Start working 4 pounds of butter to a cream and put the whites of eggs to it a spoonful at a time until it is well worked. Then put 4 pounds sugar finely powdered to it in the same manner. Then put in the yolks of the eggs and 5 pounds of flour and 5 pounds of fruit. Two hours will bake it. Add one half ounce of mace, one nutmeg, half a pint of wine and some French brandy.

The boar's head apparently never made the crossing from England, but most of the other English holiday foods were enjoyed in Virginia as well. To them were added such colonial favorites as roast turkey and eggnog, a drink made of eggs, milk, sugar, spices and rum. Although eggnog is related to the various milk and wine punches of the Old World, it seems to have been an American invention. Rum was called "grog" in the colonies, and "eggnog" probably is a corruption of "egg 'n grog."

The Christmas celebration in the slaves' cabins was far simpler, but no less eagerly awaited. Butchering time came early in December. For a few weeks there would be meat for all, including the slaves who had little but salt pork or dried fish to eat with their cornmeal the rest of the year.

Christmas Day meant gifts for everyone. The field hands gathered at the big house to receive theirs personally on Christmas morning. For the house servants a kind of game evolved. Catching any member of the owner's family, or any guest, by surprise on Christmas morning they would yell "Christmas gift!" The response was a coin or treat. This practice lasted long after slavery ended, at least in houses that still had live-in servants. Finally the custom dwindled and vanished, a discarded remnant from a different era.

The coming of winter allowed a pause in the farm work that was the center of plantation life. There were tasks to be done while waiting for planting time; land could be cleared, fences mended. But there was none of the urgency of the growing season. The field hands could have a holiday. Custom gave them the week off between Christmas and New Year's, or the time that the Yule log burned, whichever lasted longer. Bringing in the log became the slaves' privilege some time in the colonial period. They would search for the largest they could find, and if it was water-soaked, so much the better.

The week's holiday was spent in various ways. Slaves with families living on neighboring plantations were usually given leave to go to visit them. Evenings would be spent dancing and singing, days in sports of various sorts. Some of the more industrious used the time to make brooms and baskets, and sell them for money of their own. With luck a family might make three dollars. Others preferred to drink themselves into oblivion. Given a choice, most slaveholders preferred the latter occupation. Slaves who discovered they could work for themselves during the holidays might wonder why they could not do just as well the rest of the year.

Yet Christmas had a deeper meaning for these early Black Americans. Converted to Christianity, they had accepted its promise of salvation wholeheartedly. For them the real joy of Christmas was the birth at Bethlehem, and out of the period came the Christmas spirituals that are, in many ways, similar to the earliest European carols.

> Oh, Mary, what you gonna name
> That pretty little baby?
> Glory, glory, glory
> To the newborn King!

The United States, even in its earliest years, was made up of many different people. For the French in New Orleans, Christmas centered around midnight mass celebrated in the great Cathedral of St. Louis. The wealthy then went on to enjoy the *reveillon*, an elegant breakfast that lasted till almost dawn. A late dinner the next day completed the festivities. Gift-giving was lavish but it was postponed to New Year's Day —as was the endless round of calls on relatives and friends.

In the Southwest, along the Mexican border, Spanish influence predominated. The *Fiesta de la Navidad* that had been introduced by the Christian missionaries was a deeply religious day marked chiefly by attendance at mass. A crib scene, called a *nacimiento*, was found in every home. The candles of the Old World became *luminarios*, little brown paper bags weighted down with sand, and each holding a lighted candle. Gift-giving took place on January 6, the feast of the *Tres Reyes* (the Three Kings), as in Spain. That day was devoted almost exclusively to children, and a highlight of the festival was the *piñata*, a light pottery jar hung from the ceiling. Brilliantly colored and modeled in some fantastic shape, it was filled with candy, nuts and tiny presents. Each child, blindfolded, attempted to break the *piñata*. When one at least succeeded, everyone scrambled for the treats scattered over the floor.

Although the American Christmas drew upon customs of many countries, it was the influence of the German immigrants that would ultimately prove strongest of all. And Christmas was flourishing in Germany in the eighteenth and nineteenth centuries.

For the Germans it was a family celebration, affectionate and generous. There Christmas *was* for the children, and the gifts grew in number and importance. The Bavarians were the toymakers of Europe, and the Nuremberg Christmas fair, which still continues as an international toy fair, became a paradise for children. The fair, already centuries old, reached its peak in the eighteenth century. It opened in the first week of December, with a young girl dressed as an angel welcoming visitors. Hundreds of booths filled the marketplace, which was set up in the town square. Anything could be sold that pertained in some way to the coming feast, but it was primarily a toy fair.

The earliest German toys were wooden, hand-carved by people working in their own homes, much in the manner of the glassblowers of Lauscha. In the nineteenth century factories were introduced, and the mass production of toys began. Though the French were famous for their dolls, Germany retained its lead in every other type of toy-making. By 1900 Nuremberg and the neighboring town of Fuerth had some three hundred toy factories. Three-fifths of them made metal products, for the nineteenth century was the heyday of the mechanical toy. Moving birds and beasts, carousels and tricycles ran, quite literally, like clockwork. Toy trains appeared in the late 1840s, toy automobiles sixty years later. The ever-popular Teddy Bear, named for the United States president, Theodore Roosevelt, was first made at the turn of the century.

Cookies ranked second to toys in popularity, and many special kinds were baked for Christmas. Favorites included *lebkuchen* (the name means "life cakes"), dark and filled with citron; the lighter *nurnberger*, made with honey rather than molasses, and named for the "city of toys"; and *pfeffernusse* (pepper nuts), made with many different spices that sometimes, but not always, included pepper. *Spritz* (which means "spurted from a press") were rich and buttery, and anise-flavored *springerle* were made with a special *springerle* board or rolling pin that embossed distinctive designs on the top of the dough.

In the meantime, while happy German children found toys and treats under gaily trimmed and lighted trees, the day was entering a rather unattractive period in England. There Christmas in the eighteenth century lost almost all of its religious meaning. Church services were conducted, but few people attended them. Many simply spent the day playing cards. Theaters offered pantomimes and puppet shows to entertain the wealthy and their children, but the old Saturnalian ideas of gambling, eating and drinking held first place. For a laborer's family, Christmas often meant a chunk of beef, a pack of cards and a bottle of gin.

Finally in England, too, the day become more pleasant again. Queen Victoria and Prince Albert were largely responsible, for the royal couple did much more than introduce decorated trees; their lavish family celebrations soon were imitated in middle-class homes throughout the nation. Much credit must be given also to Charles Dickens, the author of *A Christmas Carol.* He wrote a number of other Christmas stories as well; none of them are read by many today—except perhaps *A Cricket on the Hearth*—but they all influenced the Christmas of his time.

Dickens's love of Christmas was real. Although his view of Christmas was not religious, it was warm, generous and sentimental. *A Christmas Carol*, written feverishly in the last few months of 1843, was not an immediate success. But when Dickens began reading his works aloud on speaking tours, the *Carol* was the favorite of his audiences. Crowds as large as thirty-five thousand, in the United States as well as in England, came to hear him speak; and he did much to break down the New England prejudice against Christmas. Miserly Scrooge, Tiny Tim and all the characters of *A Christmas Carol* live on, for the story has become a Christmas classic, widely read and dramatized in films and on television during the holiday season.

In Victorian England drinking became a less prominent feature of the day, and parlor games replaced gambling as entertainment. Blindman's buff was undoubtedly the favorite game; snapdragon the strangest. A pile of raisins were placed in a large, shallow bowl; brandy was poured over them and lighted. The object of the game was to snatch a raisin from the plate, moving quickly to avoid getting burned by the flames. A song accompanied the game:

Take care you don't take too much,
Be not greedy in your clutch,
Snip! Snap! Dragon!

With his blue and lapping tongue
Many of you will be stung,
Snip! Snap! Dragon!

For he snaps at all that comes
Snatching at his feast of plums,
Snip! Snap! Dragon!

Don't 'ee fear him, be but bold—
Out he goes, his flames are cold.
Snip! Snap! Dragon!

The game, and the scorched fingers that must have accompanied it, faded and vanished as the century came to a close.

The first Christmas card appeared in England in 1843. It was designed by John Calcott Horsley at the request of his friend Sir Henry Cole. Cole, who published illustrated books for young children, had one thousand copies printed and placed them on sale at his firm in London. Although the idea was new, there had been some forerunners. New Year's cards had been produced on the Continent since the fifteenth century, and Valentines recently had become popular in Great Britain. English firms were producing notepaper decorated with holiday symbols, to be used for Christmas letters, and Christmas "pieces" or broadsheets were commonly used by schoolchildren. The sheets had wide, decorated borders. All the child had to do was fill in a loving message and a gift was produced, ready to take home when school closed for the holidays.

Cole's card was simple. Printed on stiff cardboard and colored by hand, it showed a family party in progress. Everyone is toasting the absent friend to whom the card is addressed.

The greeting, "Merry Christmas and a Happy New Year to You," appeared below the scene, while side panels showed the poor receiving Christmas charity.

The idea of using illustrated cards to send good wishes to friends one might not see over the holidays caught on rapidly, helped by vast improvements in the postal system which came about during the same period. Many of the earliest Christmas cards resemble Valentines. Indeed, sometimes they *were* Valentines, with Christmas greetings superimposed. The picture postcard craze, which began in the latter part of the nineteenth century, greatly affected the Christmas card. For a time almost all printed Christmas greetings were in picture postcard form.

Flowers were popular subjects, and spring blossoms were as numerous as the more traditional holly and ivy. Family scenes, winter scenes, pictures of robins and wrens were plentiful. The birds shown were sometimes explicitly and unpleasantly dead. Several authorities have remembered the old Celtic custom of hunting the wren at Christmastime and speculated that there could be a connection. Ships, children and pretty girls appeared in abundance. Few pictured the Nativity or had any religious symbolism, although religion played a tremendously important part in the lives of most people at the time.

The first Christmas cards in the United States were English imports. The idea did not really take hold here until Louis Prang began producing seasonal greetings in 1875. Prang, a German immigrant, has often been called "the father of the American Christmas card." An expert lithographer, he insisted on good design. In 1880 he held the first open competitions for Christmas card designs, and noted artists began to enter the field. Competition from cheap foreign imports forced Prang to stop making cards in the 1890s, but American manufacturers again began production when World War I cut off the supply from Europe. Today the variety of Christmas cards and the closely related printed gift-wrapping paper is enormous. Choosing from the thousands of available designs is for many an important part of the preparation for Christmas.

The familiar Christmas seal originated in Denmark. A young postal clerk named Einar Holboell noticed the ever-increasing volume of Christmas mail. Saddened by the thought of the many little children who suffered from tuberculosis, he was struck by a startlingly simple idea. What if each letter and parcel carried an extra stamp, costing only one penny? The funds could go to build badly needed hospitals for those stricken with the dread disease. Full of enthusiasm, Holboell talked to everyone he met. Several prominent people expressed interest in the idea, and when King Christian himself gave his approval the success of the plan was assured. The first stamp came out during the Christmas season of 1904. Four million were sold, each bearing a portrait of Queen Louise encircled by a wreath of roses. Within a few years Sweden and Norway also adopted the plan.

Jacob Riis, a Danish immigrant to the United States who later became a crusading journalist, introduced the idea here. Riis had good reason to be interested, for six of his brothers had died of tuberculosis. The seals did not become really successful in this country until 1910, when the project was taken over by the National Tuberculosis Association. The double-barred Cross of Lorraine was selected as an emblem for the seals in 1919. Tuberculosis was the leading cause of death in the United States at the time the Christmas seal campaign began. Thanks largely to the work of the Association, it is no longer a major health problem in this country.

Eventually over forty countries adopted Einar Holboell's idea. Before he died in 1927 he had been decorated by several monarchs; he had been knighted; and he had begun to see good results come from his penny stamps.

World War I cast dark shadows over the European Christmas, but it also brought about a strange and touching tribute to the day. In 1914 the awful trenches already had been built, and war had become a way of life. Then suddenly, for one precious day and night, it stopped. The story, which first appeared in the *New York Times*, has been told a number of times, but no one, perhaps, summed it up better than an eyewitness who recalled it many years later.

> Nobody can tell you the whole true story of that incredible Christmas truce of the First World War . . . . The Germans unquestionably began it—almost certainly the Saxons . . . . Men of the North Staffordshire Regiment found themselves exchanging "words of good cheer" with their opposite numbers. Then they got up and sat on the parapet, talking across No Man's Land to each other. A British officer suggested a Volkslied [songfest]. The Germans agreed eagerly, both sides singing in turn . . . . A truce was agreed upon until midnight on Christmas Day. It took the shape at first of both sides helping one another to bury their dead.
>
> In another part of the line the troops walked about arm in arm, photographing each other, while the Germans facing a Highland Regiment began by a cornet player rendering "Home Sweet Home" perfectly, followed by a hymn tune. They then got out of their trenches and walked smilingly toward the Scots. When an officer tried to stop them they said rather pathetically—"But this is Christmas—aren't you Scotsmen Christians too?"
>
> It ended half diffidently—a gradual return to the normality of killing each other—with both sides firing warning shots in the air.

No equivalent story emerged from World War II. Not even Christmas could suspend the horror of that bloody conflict.

The first postage stamp intended especially for Christmas

use was issued by Austria in 1937. It pictured a rose, a popular Christmas symbol in that country. Brazil, two years later, issued the first stamp directly related to the story of the Nativity. It showed the three wise men and the star of Bethlehem. The first full set of stamps to illustrate the story of Christmas appeared in Hungary in 1943. One stamp showed the angels appearing to the shepherds, one the Nativity scene, and one the adoration of the Magi. Over the next fifteen years Christmas stamps appeared occasionally in one country or another.

Then the number of countries issuing Christmas stamps began to grow rapidly. In 1959 the first set of Christmas stamps from the Vatican appeared—three beautiful reproductions of Raphael's painting, *Nativity*, in different colors and denominations. The United States issued its first Christmas stamp in 1962, a small green and red stamp showing a Christmas wreath and candles. Objections that the government should not officially honor a religious holiday were voiced, but the idea seemed to be favored by many. Since 1970 some fifty nations have issued Christmas stamps annually, and designs with religious significance have proven to be the most popular.

In the twentieth century there has been an ever-increasing trend toward uniformity in the celebration of Christmas, both in Europe and in the United States. Customs that were kept for centuries in a particular area have vanished, except where they were deliberately retained, in an organized and formal manner, as a matter of local pride. An example of this sort of effort would be the Philadelphia Mummers' parade.

And the Christmas season in the United States begins earlier and earlier. For a great many children it really starts on Thanksgiving Day, when Christmas parades are held in many cities. The oldest parade is the one in New York City sponsored by Macy's department store. It has been held every year since 1927, except for three years during World War II. New York's parade, which has been televised for the last twenty-five years, has been joined by others in Philadelphia, Pennsylvania; Newark, New Jersey; Columbus, Ohio; and most recently by one in Honolulu, Hawaii, where Santa arrives on water skis.

America's high standard of living has produced the most lavish and elaborate Christmas celebrations the world has ever known. But for the poor in an affluent society, Christmas can be a difficult time. In 1971 two young Chicagoans, Kenan Heise and Arthur R. Allan, decided to find out what the day meant to harried mothers on welfare, the inmates of the county jail, the old and the lonely. The result was a little book entitled *The Death of Christmas: Interviews with Forty-Three Survivors*. All the proceeds from the sale of the book went to benefit the Neediest Families Christmas Fund. One mother told the interviewers:

> Last year, I had $7 to buy Christmas with. That didn't include any money to buy a tree. I bought my daughter a pair of mittens. The little ones, I got each a truck from the dime-store. The two big ones got 70¢ rockets that you can shoot up in the air. I was able to buy a little candy and some nuts. That was it. The $1.50 I had left bought a chicken.
>
> My children never get birthday gifts. Then, here comes all these commercials starting in September. They never tell the children how much things cost. The kids think they give them away. I'm sad when they start to advertise until Christmas is over. I hate Christmas. . . . I grew up poor and I vowed that my kids would have what I didn't.

Sadly, this, too, is Christmas.

SILENT NIGHT! HOLY NIGHT!

Silent night! holy night!
All is calm, all is bright;
Round yon Virgin Mother and Child,
Holy Infant so tender and mild:
Sleep in heavenly peace,
Sleep in heavenly peace.

Silent night! holy night!
Darkness flies, all is light;
Shepherds hear the angels sing:
Alleluia! hail the King!
Christ the Saviour is born,
Christ the Saviour is born.

Silent night! holy night!
Guiding Star, lend thy light!
See the Eastern Wise Men bring
Gifts and homage to our King!
Christ the Saviour is born,
Christ the Saviour is born.

Joseph Mohr, 1818,
translated by
John Freedman Young

The Music of Christmas

THERE WAS a renewed interest in the Christmas carol in England in the early nineteenth century. The carols, suppressed in the seventeenth century by the Christmas-hating Puritans, had survived mostly in the west of England and in Wales. In 1822 Davies Gilbert published *Some Ancient Christmas Carols, with the Tunes to which They Were Formerly Sung in the West of England*. He was followed by William Sandys, who published *Christmas Carols, Ancient and Modern* in 1833. Together Gilbert and Sandys saved such carols as "The First Nowell," "I Saw Three Ships" and "God Rest Ye Merry, Gentlemen." Both men thought of themselves as antiquarians, preserving for scholars of future generations the folk songs that were slowly dying away. Instead they inspired a revival of popular interest in carols.

In 1852 John Mason Neale, an English clergyman and hymn-writer, received a copy of *Piae cantiones*, a Swedish-German hymn collection dating from 1582. The following year Neale published *Carols for Christmastide*, "set to Ancient Melodies by the Rev. T. Helmore, M.A.: the words, principally in imitation of the original, by the Rev. J. M. Neale,

D.D." As someone has said, the imitation was not always as close as it might have been. The tune Neale used for "Good King Wenceslas" was taken from *Piae cantiones*, but originally it had been a spring carol called "Spring Has Now Unwrapped the Flowers." And Wenceslas, the hero of the newly written verses, had never been really a king; rather he was a duke, a saint and a martyr, and in his own language he would have called himself Vaclav. Ruler of Bohemia in the tenth century, Duke Vaclav was a fervent, perhaps overzealous, Christian who brought missionaries from Germany to aid in converting his people. An almost savage feudal lord, it was only in later legend that he became noted for his supposed charity. In 929 he was murdered by his pagan brother, Boleslav I, who then succeeded him as duke.

Disregarding such strange transformations, however, Neale's work did keep alive the interest roused by Gilbert and Sandys, and other scholars carried the task forward. *Christmas Carols New and Old*, the work of the Rev. H. R. Bramley and Dr. John Stainer, appeared in 1871. It was an important collection and—together with *The Oxford Book of Carols*, compiled by Percy Dearmer, R. Vaughan Williams and Martin Shaw in 1928—remains a valuable source for the true, anonymous folk carol.

Many favorite Christmas songs are not really carols, however, but hymns written in the eighteenth and nineteenth centuries. "*Adeste Fideles*" ("O Come, All Ye Faithful"), which for years was surrounded by controversy over its authorship, finally has been proven to be the work of John Francis Wade. The original manuscript is dated 1751. Wade, an Englishman, spent all his life serving as a copyist and music teacher at the Catholic seminary at Douay, in France.

Isaac Watts, a Congregationalist minister in England who began writing hymns while in his teens, wrote "Joy to the

World!" in 1719. It was a free rendering of Psalm 98. Twenty years later Charles Wesley wrote "Hark! The Herald Angels Sing." Wesley, whose brother John Wesley was the founder of Methodism, wrote more than 6,500 other hymns over the course of his lifetime. He and Watts were the most prolific hymn-writers in English history.

William C. Dix, a staid insurance company executive in nineteenth century Scotland and also an accomplished poet, wrote "What Child is This?" and "As With Gladness Men of Old." The tune used for the former came from a plaintive love ballad, usually called "Greensleeves," that was well known in Elizabethan England. "As With Gladness Men of Old" was written because Dix was distressed by the medieval legends that had grown up around the visit of the wise men described in the gospel of St. Matthew. He deliberately set out to write a hymn in which the Magi would not be kings, or three in number, or even identified in any way except as "men of old." The tune is from a German collection edited by Conrad Kocher.

A number of other well-known hymns came from the United States. "We Three Kings of Orient Are" was written by John Henry Hopkins, Jr. in 1857, while he was serving as the rector of Christ Church in Williamsport, Pennsylvania. So successfully does the hymn achieve the feeling of a folk tune that it is often assumed to be an anonymous, traditional carol, with Hopkins named merely as the "arranger."

Phillips Brooks, rector of Trinity Church, Boston, and later Episcopalian Bishop of Massachusetts, had visited the Holy Land in December, 1865. On the day before Christmas he rode on horseback from Jerusalem to Bethlehem, visiting the fields where, traditionally, the shepherds had watched their flocks. In the early evening he came upon the peaceful little village of Bethlehem.

Three years later, back in Philadelphia, Brooks wanted to

write a Christmas song for the children of his Sunday school. Remembering his visit to Bethlehem, he wrote the words to "O Little Town of Bethlehem." The church organist, Lewis Redner, wrote music for the verses. The words and tune were printed hastily on leaflets, and sung on Christmas morning by six Sunday school teachers and thirty-six children. The song was then practically forgotten until 1892 when it appeared in the hymnal of the Episcopal Church.

"I Heard the Bells on Christmas Day" was written by Henry W. Longfellow in December of 1863, as the Civil War raged on. Longfellow's son, a young lieutenant in the Union Army, had been seriously wounded and the poem, though ending on a note of hope, is filled with the author's sorrow.

Longfellow's verses have been sung to the tunes of a number of different composers. Johnny Marks, of "Rudolph, the Red-Nosed Reindeer" fame, is the latest to compose music for Longfellow's poem, and it is this version that most often is heard today.

"Away in a Manger," frequently attributed to Martin Luther, almost certainly was not written by him, as it is virtually unknown in Germany. Instead, it seems to have originated among the German Lutherans in Pennsylvania. It first appeared in print in *A Little Children's Book for Schools and Families*, published in 1885.

But the world's best-loved Christmas song, "Silent Night," came not from England or the United States but from Austria. It was written on Christmas Eve, 1818, in the little village of Oberndorf, near Salzburg.

The organ in the village church had broken down because a mouse had gnawed away at the bellows, and the young assistant pastor, Joseph Mohr, was distressed. The organ could not possibly be mended in time for midnight mass, and Christmas without music would not seem like Christmas at all. On impulse,

Mohr decided to write something new. Perhaps Franz Gruber, the organist, could come up with a simple tune that could be played on the guitar. Gruber, who was also the schoolmaster at the nearby village of Arnsdorf, received the poem from Father Mohr some time that afternoon, and set to work at once. By evening he had a melody arranged for two solo voices, chorus and guitar accompaniment. The song was sung that night. If the congregation was surprised to hear a guitar at mass, they were nevertheless grateful that the two men had gone to so much effort, and the incident was forgotten.

Finally, weeks later, the organ-mender arrived. He heard of the song so hastily written for Christmas Eve and asked for a copy of it. Here the story of the carol becomes blurred. The organ-mender evidently passed his copy on to a number of people. The song become widely known when it was adopted by two groups of Tyrolese singers, the Strassers and the more professional Rainers; but the names of Mohr and Gruber were forgotten. Finally, in 1854, an official inquiry was sent to the church in Salzburg. Rumor had it that the song had been written by Franz Joseph Haydn's son Michael. Did the church perhaps have records that would settle the matter once and for all?

Chance again played a part. Franz Gruber's son Felix was serving as a choirboy at the church. Hearing of the inquiry, he insisted that his father, not the well-known Haydn, was the composer. The elder Gruber, who had been content to be ignored for more than thirty-five years, submitted a signed statement and the matter was finally settled.

The hymn, so hastily improvised in an out-of-the-way village, has since been translated into more than ninety different languages and dialects.

But Christmas is a theme that has inspired the greatest of musicians as well as little-known composers. Johann Sebastian Bach, a deeply religious man who came from a long line of musicians, wrote his *Christmas Oratorio* in 1733. It was performed for the first time in Leipzig, Germany, the following year. It was Bach himself who called it an oratorio, which generally implies a unified work to be performed at a single hearing. Really, however, it was a series of six cantatas to be sung at Lutheran church services on Christmas and the two days following, and then on New Year's Day, the Sunday following New Year's, and Epiphany. Each part is complete in itself, yet they are linked together by chorales which provide a unity of subject and design. In modern performances usually only the first three cantatas are sung, which give the complete story of the Nativity as told by St. Luke. Part four tells of the naming of Jesus, and parts five and six relate the story of the Magi. Bach is considered one of the finest organists and composers of all time, and the music is magnificent when properly performed.

George Frederick Handel, like Bach an extremely gifted German composer and musician, left his patron, the Elector of Hanover, in 1712 to go to London. A year later the English Queen Anne died, and young Handel was dismayed to realize that his deserted benefactor would now be King George I of England. The king at first refused to see him. Later a reconciliation took place, and Handel stayed in his adopted homeland, devoting himself to opera. Plagued by financial difficulties, he eventually turned to oratorios and produced a number of excellent works based on the Old Testament, all of which were intended for stage performances.

Handel began work on his most famous oratorio, the *Messiah*, in August of 1741, and completed the entire work in twenty-three days. The text was taken directly from the words of the New Testament, and the libretto was arranged by Charles Jennings.

Invited to Dublin by the Duke of Devonshire, who was then Lord Lieutenant of Ireland, Handel arranged to have his work introduced at a benefit performance in a theater there. The Anglo-Irish aristocracy was delighted. So great was the demand for seats that the managers of the theater asked the gentlemen to leave their swords at home and the ladies to refrain from wearing the hoops that normally held out their full skirts, so that more people could be seated at each performance.

Handel returned to London where the *Messiah* was again performed on the stage, but now the composer found his work severely criticized. Proper Londoners were aghast to hear theater folk of presumably dubious reputations singing about the life of Christ. As a result, Handel rarely produced the *Messiah*, though its performance did become an annual event as a benefit for the London Foundling Hospital. Here the charitable motive silenced all opposition.

Almost exactly one and a half centuries after Handel wrote his famous oratorio, another great composer, Peter Ilich Tchaikovsky, began work on the music for a new Christmas ballet, *The Nutcracker.* Tchaikovsky, a Russian musician whose work was far more favorably received abroad than at home, based his ballet on E. T. A. Hoffman's tale, "The Nutcracker and the Mouse-king." A nutcracker was a popular toy for a child at the time. Made to resemble an ugly little man, it had a grotesque jaw which could be opened to crack nuts.

An elaborate scenario was prepared by Marius Petipa, who also produced the ballet. In it the nutcracker is given to two children, Clara and Fritz, on Christmas Eve. Later in the night the nutcracker leads the dolls and toy soldiers in a battle against the mice. He then turns into a handsome prince who takes Clara into an enchanted kingdom where they find the Sugar Plum Fairy.

The music Tchaikovsky wrote for this tale has delighted generations of both children and adults, but he himself took little pleasure in it. He told a friend, "I began the ballet with an effort, sensing a decline in my inventive powers." Despite the immediate success of *The Nutcracker* when it was presented to the public in 1892, he remained convinced that it was "far weaker than *The Sleeping Beauty*" and not nearly as well done as his other earlier ballet, *Swan Lake*.

In recent years the magic of television has brought *The Nutcracker* to many thousands of children who might never have seen it on the stage, and for a growing number of families the performance has become an eagerly anticipated part of the holiday season.

Television can be given credit for the very creation of another Christmas classic. In 1951 the National Broadcasting Company commissioned Gian Carlo Menotti to write a new Christmas opera to be broadcast in December of that year. Menotti, an American composer of Italian birth, was wandering through the Metropolitan Museum of Art, in New York City, when he chanced upon the painting "Adoration of the Kings" by Hieronymus Bosch. Deciding that his topic would be the journey of the Magi, he wrote *Amahl and the Night Visitors*, an opera in one act which was broadcast on December 24, 1951. The popularity of the work has grown; it seems that Menotti has produced yet another American addition to the traditional Christmas scene.

For there is no setting limits on what will become a part of Christmas. "Jingle Bells," written by James Pierpont in 1857, never once mentions the day, yet it has become a favorite holiday song. Despite the cheerful simplicity of his song, Pierpont's own life was a mass of contradictions. The son of a prominent abolitionist, he nevertheless moved to Georgia, married a Southern girl and served in the Confederate Army. Plagued by money difficulties most of his life, he lived to see his nephew John Pierpont Morgan become one of the wealthiest people in the United States.

Another favorite Christmas song that does not fit easily into any particular category is "The Twelve Days of Christmas." It cannot be considered a true carol, for it is undoubtedly pagan and magical in origin; counting songs almost always are. An early French version lists as gifts: a good stuffing without bones, two breasts of veal, three joints of beef, four pigs' trotters, five legs of mutton, six partridges with cabbage, seven spitted rabbits, eight plates of salad, nine dishes from the chapter-house, ten full casks, eleven beautiful maidens and twelve musketeers with their swords. Numerous variations can be found.

The first known English version appeared in a tiny nursery book called *Mirth Without Mischief*, which was printed in 1780. During the Victorian period it became not so much a song as a parlor game. Those who could not remember the various gifts surrendered a forfeit of some sort.

The version so well known today was published by J. O. Helliwell in England in 1842. The first seven days' presents are all birds, for the five gold rings refer to the five golden bands of the ring-necked pheasant. The four colly birds, often corrupted to four calling birds, are blackbirds.

Although known in the United States, "The Twelve Days of Christmas" was rarely heard until the 1940s. Since that time it has become ever more popular, both as a song and as a Christmas theme.

"The Little Drummer Boy," featured on countless Christmas cards and known to almost everyone, is a recent addition to Christmas. The song was written by Katherine Kennicott Davis in the early 1940s. As she herself has related, the music came first, and "the words seemed to come along with it. The drumming idea seemed to suit it—it is a device that one finds particularly in French folksongs, and I had used it before."

At the time Davis, a professional songwriter, was working on numerous songs for school books. This tune was given the title "Carol of the Drum," and listed simply as "Czech," as if it were a traditional melody.

In the late 1950s another publisher brought out a new version, with slight changes in both words and music, and Harry Simeone recorded it under the title "The Little Drummer Boy." The song became a hit in 1959, and a number of televised versions appeared. A lawsuit established Davis as the original author, but the public, entranced by both story and tune, cared little either way.

"White Christmas," written by Irving Berlin, is another relatively new Christmas song. It was first sung by Bing Crosby in the motion picture *Holiday Inn.* The film was released in August 1942, and the song became an immediate hit. The United States had entered World War II the previous December and "White Christmas," as Berlin said years later, "became a peace song in wartime," echoing the nostalgia of thousands of homesick soldiers. Over the next twenty-five years more than 135,000,000 records were sold, more than any other single recording.

And so the age-old practice of absorbing and adapting goes on and on. Christmas after so many centuries is like a giant snowball rolling downhill. It gathers many things to itself, and lets go of very little. The "babe, wrapped in swaddling cloths and lying in a manger" remains the central figure, but other motifs come and, more rarely, go. The candle, the wreath and the mistletoe are ancient, the reindeer and the poinsettia far more recent.

The symbols vary, but the message remains the same—joy, peace, love and generosity. Merry Christmas!

Bibliography

The Holy Bible: Revised Standard Version containing the Old and New Testaments translated from the original tongues, being the version set forth A.D. 1611, *revised A.D.* 1881-1885 *and A.D.* 1901, *compared with the most ancient authorities and revised A.D.* 1952. New York: Thomas Nelson and Sons, 1952.

BUDAY, GEORGE. *The History of the Christmas Card.* London: Spring Books, 1954.

CAGNER, EWERT (comp.). *Swedish Christmas.* Translated by Yvonne Aboav-Elmquist. New York: Henry Holt and Company, 1959.

CHAMBERS, EDMUND K. *The Medieval Stage.* 2 vols. London: Oxford University Press, 1903.

CHAMBERS, ROBERT (ed.). *The Book of Days: A Miscellany of Popular Antiquities in Connection with the Calendar.* 2 vols. Reprint of the 1862-64 edition. Detroit: Gale Research Company, 1967.

COUNT, EARL W. *4000 Years of Christmas.* New York: Henry Schuman, 1948.

CRIPPEN, THOMAS G. *Christmas and Christmas Lore.* London: Blackie and Son, 1923.

CROFT, ALOYIUS (ed.). *The Mystery of Christmas.* Milwaukee: The Bruce Publishing Company, 1956.

DANIELOU, JEAN. *The Infancy Narratives.* Translated by Rosemary Sheed. New York: Herder and Herder, 1968.

DAWSON, WILLIAM. *Christmas: Its Origin and Associations, Together with Its Historical Events and Festive Celebrations during Nineteen Centuries.* Reprint of the 1902 edition. Detroit: Gale Research Company, 1968.

DEARMER, PERCY; WILLIAMS, RALPH VAUGHAN; and SHAW, MARTIN (eds.). *The Oxford Book of Carols.* London: Oxford University Press, 1928.

DOUGLAS, GEORGE WILLIAM. *The American Book of Days.* Revised by Helen Douglas Compton. New York: The H. W. Wilson Company, 1948.

EBON, MARTIN. *Saint Nicholas: Life and Legend.* New York: Harper and Row, Publishers, 1975.

EHRET, WALTER, and EVANS, GEORGE K. (comps.). *The International Book of Christmas Carols.* Englewood Cliffs, N.J.: Prentice Hall, Inc., 1963.

FOLEY, DANIEL. *The Christmas Tree.* Philadelphia: Chilton Book Company, 1960.

FRAZER, JAMES GEORGE. *The Golden Bough: A Study in Magic and Religion.* Abridged edition. New York: The Macmillan Company, 1922.

GALLICO, PAUL. *The Story of Silent Night.* New York: Crown Publishers, Inc., 1967.

GRAY, LOUIS HERBERT (ed.). *The Mythology of All Races.* 13 vols. New York: Cooper Square Publishers, Inc., 1964.

GRIMM, JACOB. *Teutonic Mythology*. Translated by James Steven Stallybrass. 4 vols. Reprint of the 1883-1888 edition. New York: Dover Publications, Inc., 1966.

HASTINGS, JAMES (ed.). *Encyclopaedia of Religion and Ethics*. 13 vols. New York: Charles Scribner's Sons, 1908-1926.

HADFIELD, MILES AND JOHN. *Twelve Days of Christmas*. Boston: Little, Brown and Company, 1961.

HAWKES, JACQUETTA. *Man and the Sun*. New York: Random House, 1962.

HOLE, CHRISTINA. *Christmas and Its Customs*. New York: M. Barrows and Company, Inc., 1957.

JAMES, EDWIN OLIVER. *Seasonal Feasts and Festivals*. New York: Barnes and Noble, Inc., 1961.

JOHNSTON, LESLIE DENT. "Classical Origins of Christmas Customs." Unpublished Ph.D. dissertation, University of Illinois, 1936.

JONES, E. WILLIS. *The Santa Claus Book*. New York: Walker and Company, 1976.

KANE, HARNETT T. *The Southern Christmas Book*. New York: David McKay Company, Inc., 1958.

LANG, PAUL HENRY. *George Frideric Handel*. New York: W. W. Norton and Company, Inc., 1966.

LAWRENCE, MARY (comp.). *Mother and Child: 100 Works of Art with Commentaries by 106 Distinguished People*. New York: Thomas Y. Crowell Company, 1975.

MCNEILL, FLORENCE MARIAN. *The Silver Bough: a Four Volume Study of the National and Local Festivals of Scotland*. Glasgow: William Maclellan, 1957.

MAIER, PAUL L. *First Christmas: The True and Unfamiliar Story*. New York: Harper and Row, Publishers, 1971.

METCALFE, EDNA. *The Trees of Christmas.* New York: Abingdon Press, 1961.

MILES, CLEMENT A. *Christmas in Ritual and Tradition, Christian and Pagan.* Reprint of the 1912 edition. Detroit: Gale Research Company, 1968.

O'SHEA, DENIS. *The First Christmas.* Milwaukee: The Bruce Publishing Company, 1952.

PAINE, ALBERT BIGELOW. *Thomas Nast: His Period and His Pictures.* Reprint of the 1904 edition. Princeton, N.J.: Pyne Press, 1974.

PATTERSON, SAMUEL WHITE. *The Poet of Christmas Eve: A Life of Clement Clarke Moore, 1779-1863.* New York: Morehouse-Gorham Company, Inc., 1956.

PITLUGA, LINTON and PHYLLIS. *The Christmas Star.* Chicago: Cygnus Publishing Company, 1976.

RAGGIO, OLGA. *The Nativity: The Christmas Creche at the Metropolitan Museum of Art.* Garden City, N.Y.: Doubleday and Company, Inc., 1965.

RICCIOTTI, GIUSEPPE. *The Life of Christ.* Translated by Alba I. Zizzamia. Milwaukee: The Bruce Publishing Company, 1947.

ROLLINS, CHARLEMAE (comp.). *Christmas Gif': An Anthology of Christmas Poems, Songs and Stories, Written by and about Negroes.* Chicago: Follett Publishing Company, 1963.

SHEKERJIAM, HAIG AND REGINA. (comps.). *A Book of Christmas Carols.* New York: Harper and Row, Publishers, 1963.

SNYDER, PHILIP. *The Christmas Tree Book: A History of the American Christmas Tree and Its Ornaments.* New York: The Viking Press, 1976.

SPICER, DOROTHY GLADYS. *Festivals of Western Europe.* New York: H. W. Wilson Company, 1958.

TEMPLE, PATRICK J. *Pattern Divine or Our Lord's Hidden Life.* St. Louis, Mo.: B. Herder Book Company, 1950.

TENNANT, EUGENIA L. *American Christmases: From the Puritans to the Victorians.* Hicksville, N.Y.: Exposition Press, Inc., 1975.

WALLACE, ROBERT. *The World of Leonardo, 1452-1519.* New York: Time Incorporated, 1966.

WALSH, WILLIAM S. *Curiosities of Popular Customs.* Philadelphia: J.B. Lippincott Company, 1897.

WARRACK, JOHN. *Tchaikovsky.* New York: Charles Scribner's Sons, 1973.

WEISER, FRANCIS X. *Handbook of Christian Feasts and Customs: The Year of the Lord in Liturgy and Folklore.* New York: Harcourt, Brace and Company, 1952.

______. *The Christmas Book.* New York: Harcourt, Brace and Company, 1952.

WERNECKE, HERBERT H. *Christmas Songs and Their Stories.* Philadelphia: The Westminster Press, 1957.

YOUNG, JOANNE B. *Christmas in Williamsburg.* Williamsburg, Va.: The Colonial Williamsburg Foundation, 1970.

Index